Workbook

German

False beginners

Bettina Schödel

Adapted for English speakers
by Paul Gerard Pickering

About this workbook

The 21 lessons in this workbook, which contain some 240 exercises, will allow you to progressively review and practice the fundamentals of German, from pronunciation and grammar through to useful vocabulary and expressions.

Each lesson deals with a key grammatical point such as verb conjugation, declension or sentence structure (yellow panels), as well as giving pronunciation and spelling tips (pink panels). Key vocabulary and expressions are also included (green panels). The exercises allow active and contextual reinforcement of the points covered, calling upon your knowledge of the language. Verb conjugation and declension tables are found before the answer section at the back. The aim of the workbook is to provide a fun and systematic way to consolidate your German skills.

If it has been over a decade since you last studied German, you may notice certain spelling differences (e.g. **wie viel** instead of **wieviel** or **dass** instead of **daß**). These are the result of a series of spelling reforms, the latest of which took effect in 2006.

As you work through the lessons, you can self-assess your results by selecting the appropriate icon after each exercise (☺ if the majority of your answers were correct, ☹ if around half your answers were correct, or ☹ if less than half were correct). After a lesson, enter the number of icons of each type you received in the exercises, and then enter these totals into the final score table at the end of the workbook so you can tally your final results after completing all the exercises.

Contents

1. The present tense 3–7
2. The imperative 8–13
3. The present perfect 14–19
4. The simple past 20–25
5. The future...................................... 26–29
6. The subjunctive II 30–35
7. The passive voice.............................. 36–41
8. Nouns & the nominative 42–47
9. The accusative................................. 48–53
10. The dative 54–59
11. The genitive.................................. 60–63
12. Two-way prepositions 64–69
13. Word order.................................... 70–75

14. Modal verbs.................................... 76–79
15. Verbs with prefixes 80–85
16. Prepositional verbs 86–91
17. Infinitives 92–97
18. Showing possession 98–103
19. Relative pronouns............................ 104–109
20. Making comparisons 110–115
21. Numbers...................................... 116–117
Verb conjugation tables 118–119
Declension tables 120–121
Answers 122–127
Self-assessment 128

The present tense

The present tense

- The present tense is used in the same way as in English, with two notable differences. German does not have progressive/continuous tenses (*to be + ...-ing*), so the present tense is used to express a current continuous action: **Ich komme.** *I am coming* ('I come'). The present tense is also very often used to express a future event: **Er kommt morgen zurück.** *He is coming* ('comes') *back tomorrow.*

- Regular conjugation endings: **kommen** *to come* (infinitives end in **-en** or **-n**) ➜ **ich komme, du kommst, er/sie/es kommt, wir kommen, ihr kommt, sie/Sie kommen**.

- The subject pronouns are **ich** *I*, **du** *you* (informal sing.), **er** *he, it* (m.), **sie** *she, it* (f.), **es** *it* (n.), **wir** *we*, **ihr** *you* (informal pl.), **sie** *they*, **Sie** *you* (formal).

- One of the main changes from the regular conjugation pattern in most irregular (or 'strong') verbs is a vowel change in the <u>second- and third-person singular</u> present tense (typically **a ➜ ä** or **e ➜ i / ie**): **schlafen** *to sleep* ➜ **du schläfst, er/sie/es schläft**; **geben** *to give* ➜ **du gibst, er/sie/es gibt**.

- The conjugations of **haben** *to have*, **sein** *to be* and **werden** *to become* are irregular.

I Complete this table with the correct present tense forms.

	ich	du	er/sie/es	wir	ihr	sie/Sie
wohnen		wohnst				
beginnen			beginnt			
fragen						fährst
fahren		fährst				
laufen				laufen		
nehmen					nehmt	

2 Indicate whether these verbs are regular (R), i.e. no vowel change, or irregular (IR). For the irregular verbs, give the third-person singular form of the present tense.

E.g. sprechen → (IR) er/sie/es spricht

a. sehen → ....

b. hoffen → ....

c. schlafen → ....

d. fallen → ....

e. glauben → ....

f. gehen → ....

g. sagen → ....

h. treffen → ....

3 Complete this table with the correct present tense forms.

ich	du	er/sie/es	wir	ihr	sie/Sie
bin	....	....	sind	....	....
....	hast	....	....	habt	....
werde	....	wird	....	....	werden

4 Complete the following sentences using these verbs in the present tense.

empfehlen **sprechen** **finden** **grüßen** **lesen** **bitten**

a. Ich .... meine Brille nicht. Weißt du, wo sie ist?

b. Welche Zeitung .... Sie da?

c. Ich .... dich um deine Hilfe.

d. Er ist schon seit einer Stunde am Telefon. Mit wem .... er denn so lange?

e. Dieser Mann ist so unfreundlich. Er .... mich nie.

f. Was .... du mir? Fisch oder Fleisch?

5 Turn these nouns into verbs and conjugate them in the third-person singular present tense. E.g. die Miete → mieten → er/sie/es mietet

a. die Sprache → .... → ....
b. die Schrift → .... → ....
c. das Getränk → .... → ....
d. die Liebe → .... → ....
e. der Flug → .... → ....
f. die Reparatur → .... → ....

Some spelling and pronunciation tips

• In the present tense, verb stems (i.e. after the removal of the infinitive **-en/-n** ending) that end in **-d** or **-t** or certain other consonant groups such as **-chn** or **-tm** have a spelling change from the regular conjugation. In these verbs, an **e** is inserted before the conjugation ending in the second- and third-person singular and the second-person plural to make the pronunciation easier: **arbeiten** *to work* → **du arbeitest, er/sie/es arbeitet, ihr arbeitet**. If the verb has a vowel change, only the second-person plural takes an **e**: **halten** *to hold* → **du hältst, er/sie/es hält, ihr haltet**.

• Verb stems ending in **-s, -ss, -ß, -tz** or **-z** take only a **-t** (rather than **-st**) in the second-person singular: **blasen** *to blow* → **du bläst**.

• Infinitives ending in **-eln** or **-ern** take only an **-n** (rather than **-en**) in the first- and third-person plural: **sammeln** *to gather* → **wir sammeln, sie/Sie sammeln**. In these verbs, the **e** of the verb stem in the first-person singular is often omitted, although this is not obligatory: **ich samm(e)le**.

6 Complete the table with the correct present tense forms.

	ich	du	er/sie/es	wir	ihr	sie/Sie
baden						
reisen						
wechseln						

7 Conjugate these verbs in the present for the persons indicated.

a. antworten *(second-person plural)* → ....
b. zeichnen *(third-person singular)* → ....
c. verändern *(third-person plural)* → ....
d. lesen *(second-person singular)* → ....

Formal and informal address

- German has different ways to say *you* depending on who is being addressed. With children, friends and family, the informal *you* is used: **du** for one person (second-person singular) or **ihr** for more than one person (second-person plural). In most other cases, it is polite to use the formal **Sie** (capitalized) for addressing one or more people. The formal *you* always conjugates in the third-person plural.

- Certain forms of greeting vary depending on whether the context is informal or formal. **Hallo!** *Hi!* and **Tschüss!** *See you!* are more friendly and casual, while **Guten Tag!** *Hello!* ('Good day!') and **Auf Wiedersehen!** *Goodbye!* are more formal (however, this is not a hard and fast rule – you might hear any of these greetings in a variety of contexts).

- In German-speaking countries, titles still matter, so they need to be included in formal contexts: **Herr Professor Bachmann**, **Frau Doktor Schmidt**.

8 Translate these questions using *Zeit haben*.

a. Do you have time? *(formal)* → ....

b. Do you have time? *(informal sing.)* → ....

c. Do you have time? *(informal pl.)* → ....

d. Do they have time? → ....

9 Rewrite these greetings for two different contexts: addressing a couple of close friends and addressing an older stranger.

Informal singular	Informal plural	Formal
Hallo, wer bist du?		
Wie heißt du? – Paul, und du?		
Woher kommst du?		
Wo wohnst du?		
Wie lange bist du schon in Berlin?		
Schön, dass du gekommen bist.		
Tschüss!		

 Complete the greetings with these words.

a. Bis ....! *(See you soon!)*

b. Bis ....! *(See you tomorrow!)*

c. Bis ....! *(See you later!)*

d. Gute ....! *(Good night!)*

e. Bis ....! *(See you in a minute!)*

Nacht

morgen

bald

später

gleich

The case of pronouns

In German, a pronoun declines (changes form) depending on its function in the sentence. If it is the subject of the sentence, it is in the **nominative** case; if it is a direct object, it is in the **accusative**; and if it is an indirect object, it is in the **dative**. If the pronoun is used in a short phrase, the case depends on the implied full sentence.

- **Ich habe Hunger. – Ich auch!** *I'm hungry. – Me too!*
  Implied: **Ich habe auch Hunger!** → nominative

- **Es ärgert mich! – Mich auch!** *That annoys me. – Me too!*
  Implied: **Es ärgert mich auch!** → accusative

- **Mir gefällt es. – Mir nicht!** *That appeals to me. – Not to me!*
  Implied: **Mir gefällt es nicht!** → dative

Complete the sentences with the appropriate pronoun (for personal pronoun declensions, see p. 120).

a. *I come from Munich. And you?* (informal plural)
   → Ich komme aus München. Und ....?

b. *I'm glad. – Me too!*
   → Es freut mich! – .... auch!

c. *I like the taste. Don't you?* (informal singular)
   → Mir schmeckt es. .... nicht!

d. *I'm coming. You too?* (informal singular)
   → Ich komme mit. .... auch!

e. *I like it very much. And you?* (formal)
   → Es hat mir sehr gut gefallen. Und ....?

Well done! You've reached the end of Lesson 1. It's time to count up how many of each type of icon you received. Then record your results in the final self-assessment table on page 128.

2

The imperative

The imperative

- The imperative is the verb form used for commands or requests. In German, there are different forms depending on whether you are addressing someone informally (**du** for one person or **ihr** for more than one person) or formally (**Sie**). There is also a **wir** (first-person plural) form, which translates in English to *Let's …!*

- Here are the regular conjugation endings: **tanzen** *to dance* → **Tanz(e)!** (informal sing.) **Tanzen wir!** *Let's dance!* **Tanzt!** (informal pl.) **Tanzen Sie!** (formal). Note that the **-e** of the **du** command is optional: **Tanz!** or **Tanze!** are both correct. The **wir** and **Sie** commands must include the subject pronouns after the verb.

  One common irregular verb is **sein** *to be* → **Sei! Seien wir! Seid! Seien Sie! Sei ruhig!** *Be quiet!* (informal sing.)

- Irregular verbs whose vowel changes from **e → i / ie** in the present tense also have this change in the **du** command: **geben** *to give* → **du gibst** *you give* → **Gib!** *Give!*

- In separable-prefix verbs (see Lesson 15), the prefix goes to the end of the command, e.g. **losfahren** *to drive off* → **Fahr los! / Fahr jetzt los!** *Drive off now!*

- In negative commands (prohibitions), **nicht** comes after the verb, or after the subject pronoun for **wir** and **Sie** commands: **Komm nicht zu spät nach Hause! / Kommen Sie nicht zu spät nach Hause!** *Don't come home too late!*

1 Turn these verbs or phrases into commands.

a. kommen *(informal pl.)* → ....

b. nicht zu laut singen *(informal sing.)* → ....

c. an/rufen* *(first-person plural)* → ....

d. das Buch lesen *(informal pl.)* → ....

e. spazieren gehen *(first-person plural)* → ....

f. da bleiben *(formal)* → ....

g. mit/kommen* *(informal pl.)* → ....

h. Blumen kaufen *(informal sing.)* → ....

*separable-prefix verb

2 Use the following verb phrases to form these commands.

bitte pünktlich sein   nicht traurig sein

nett zu ihr sein   ehrlich sein   vorsichtig sein

a. Please be on time! *(informal singular)* → ....

b. Let's be honest! → ....

c. Be nice to her! *(informal plural)* → ....

d. Don't be sad! *(formal)* → ....

e. Be careful! *(informal singular)* → ....

3 Connect these commands to their translations.

1. Pass auf!   •   • **a.** Stop!

2. Fahr weiter!   •   • **b.** Come with [me/us]!

3. Geh weg!   •   • **c.** Go away!

4. Sprich leiser!   •   • **d.** Speak more quietly!

5. Komm mit!   •   • **e.** Continue driving!

6. Hör auf!   •   • **f.** Watch out!

7. Halt an!   •   • **g.** Stop [the car]!

4 Complete the opposite of each command using the appropriate prefix/adverb: *rückwärts, weniger, runter, zu, aus.* Then connect each to its translation.

1. Steig ein! ≠ Steig ....! •

                       • **a.** Eat more! ≠ Eat less!

2. Fahr vorwärts! ≠ Fahr ....! •

                       • **b.** Get in! ≠ Get out! *(car, bus, etc.)*

3. Komm hoch! ≠ Komm ....! •

                       • **c.** Open the door! ≠ Close the door!

4. Iss mehr! ≠ Iss ....! •

                       • **d.** Come up! ≠ Come down!

5. Mach die Tür auf!

   ≠ Mach die Tür ....! •

                       • **e.** Go forward! ≠ Go back!

Some spelling and pronunciation tips

- In the imperative, verb stems that end in **-d** or **-t** or certain other consonant groups such as **-chn** or **-tm** generally insert an **e** before the conjugation ending in the second-person plural (**ihr**) command: **zeichnen** *to draw* → **Zeichnet einen Hund!** In the second-person singular (**du**) command, the **-e** that is optional in other verbs is typically included: **Zeichne einen Hund!** (However, in strong verbs, this **e** is optional whatever the verb stem, e.g. **Lad(e) ihn ein!** *Invite him!*)

- Infinitives ending in **-ern** or **-eln** always include the **-e** in the second-person singular (**du**) command: **wackeln** *to wiggle* → **Wack(e)le nicht so!** In most cases, the **e** of the stem is omitted (e.g. **Wackle!**), although this is not obligatory.

5 Complete this table with the correct imperative forms.

Informal sing. (du)	Informal plural (ihr)
....	Arbeitet schneller!
Verändere nichts!	....
Bade nicht jetzt!	....
....	Ärgert mich nicht!
....	Wechselt 100 Euro!
Lad(e) ihn ein!	....

Zu Befehl!
Yes, sir!

6 Change these formal *Sie* commands to informal *du* and *ihr* commands. Keep in mind the spelling tips!

a. Finden Sie es sofort! → ....

b. Schreiben Sie es auf! → ....

c. Lassen Sie mich in Ruhe! → ....

d. Schneiden Sie es in zwei! → ....

e. Steigen Sie bitte ein! → ....

f. Haben Sie etwas Geduld! → ....

Interjections and exclamations

Some exclamations are very similar in German and English, e.g. **Super!** or **Wunderbar!**
But others are totally different, e.g. **Toll!** or **Prima!** *Great!* Other useful terms include
Gesundheit! *Bless you!* after someone sneezes (literally, 'Health'!), **Prost!** *Cheers!*
before clinking glasses, and **Quatsch!** *Rubbish! Nonsense!*

7 Connect the exclamations.

1. Aua!/Auatsch! •   • **a**. Ugh! Yuck!

2. Bäh!/Pfui!/Igitt! •   • **b**. Hooray!

3. Uff! •   • **c**. Good luck!

4. Hurra! •   • **d**. Oh, I see!

5. Ach so! •   • **e**. There you are! You see?

6. Na also! •   • **f**. Phew!

7. Toi, toi, toi! •   • **g**. Ouch!

8 Connect the exclamations.

1. Zum Glück! •   • **a**. What a shame!

2. Schade! •   • **b**. Thank God!

3. Gott sei Dank! •   • **c**. Wow!

4. Gesundheit! •   • **d**. Cheers!

5. Mensch! •   • **e**. Enjoy your meal!

6. Prost! Zum Wohl!•   • **f**. Bless you!

7. Guten Appetit! •   • **g**. Fortunately!

9 Unscramble the letters to find the German equivalent of these exclamations.

a. Quiet! **U/H/R/E**

→ ....

b. Watch out! **C/H/N/G/U/T/A**

→ ....

c. Get out! **U/S/R/A**

→ ....

d. Let's go! **O/S/L**

→ ....

Some nature vocabulary

Don't confuse **der See** *lake* and **die See** *sea*, an excellent example of why knowing the grammatical gender of a noun is important! Germany is bordered by two seas, **die Nordsee** *the North Sea* and **die Ostsee** *the Baltic Sea*. If you visit these beaches, you might want to make use of **ein Strandkorb** (literally, 'beach-basket'). These are big beach chairs fitted with a hood for protection from the elements!

10 Translate the following words into German or English.

a. forest → der ....

b. tree → der ....

c. leaf → das ....

d. flower → die ....

e. sea* → das ....

f. .... → der Strand

g. sand → der ....

h. .... → die Welle

i. mountain → der ....

j. .... → der Bach

k. .... → das Gras

l. .... → der Stein

m. .... → der Bauernhof

n. animal → das ....

o. .... → der Stall

p. .... → das Feld

*(a word other than **See**)

11 Connect each verb to its translation.

1. tauchen •
2. Ski fahren •
3. wandern •
4. bergsteigen •
5. reiten •
6. segeln •

• **a.** horse riding
• **b.** mountain climbing
• **c.** (scuba) diving
• **d.** sailing
• **e.** hiking
• **f.** skiing

12 Fill in the missing vowels in these translations.

a. lion → der **L _ W _**

b. cat → die **K _ TZ _**

c. pig → das **SCHW _ _ N**

d. sheep → das **SCH _ F**

e. butterfly → der **SCHM _ TT _ RL _ NG**

f. mosquito → die **M _ CK _**

g. bird → der **V _ G _ L**

h. mouse → die **M _ _ S**

i. cow → die **K _ H**

j. wolf → der **W _ LF**

k. giraffe → die **G _ R _ FF _**

l. ant → die **_ M _ _ S _**

m. horse → das **PF _ RD**

n. hare → der **H _ S _**

o. fish → der **F _ SCH**

p. bee → die **B _ _ N _**

q. spider → die **SP _ NN _**

r. wasp → die **W _ SP _**

 Unscramble the letters to translate these verbs. ..

a. to bark **N/L/B/E/L/E**

→ ....

b. to meow **I/U/A/M/N/E**

→ ....

c. to swim **M/C/I/S/H/W/E/M/N**

→ ....

d. to fly **L/F/G/I/N/E/E**

→ ....

e. to roar **N/B/L/L/R/Ü/E**

→ ....

f. to sting **T/H/N/S/E/E/C**

→ ....

Animal-related expressions

Many German idiomatic expressions make reference to animals. Interestingly, often the equivalent English expression also refers to an animal, but a different one, or the same animal but doing something different! E.g. *I'll believe it when pigs fly.* = **Ich glaub, mein Schwein pfeift!** ('I believe my pig whistles!'). In some cases, the English expression uses a completely different metaphor.

Can you find the equivalent English expressions? ..

a. einen Frosch im Hals haben ('to have a frog in the throat')

→ ....

b. einen Bärenhunger haben ('to have a bear's hunger')

→ ....

c. bekannt sein wie ein bunter Hund ('to be as well-known as a coloured dog')

→ ....

d. zwei Fliegen mit einer Klappe schlagen ('to hit two flies with one flap')

→ ....

Excellent! You've reached the end of Lesson 2. Count up the icons from the exercises and record your result in the final evaluation table on page 128.

3

The present perfect

The present perfect

- As in English, this tense is used to express a completed action that has a relationship with the present. However, today there is an increasing tendency in spoken German to use it instead of the simple past (see Lesson 4) to relate anything that happened in the past, even if the action is definitively completed.

- The present perfect is a two-word (or compound) tense formed with the auxiliary verb **haben** *to have* (or in some cases, **sein**) conjugated in the present tense + past participle. The past participle is placed at the end of the clause:
Ich habe ihn gesehen. *I have seen him.*

- The past participle of most regular (weak) verbs is formed by adding the prefix **ge-** and the suffix **-t** to the verb stem: **mach**en → **ge**mach**t**. If the verb stem ends in **-d** or **-t** or the consonant groups **-chn**, **-tm**, the suffix is **-et**: **arbeit**en → **ge**arbeit**et**.

- The past participle of most irregular (strong) verbs is **ge-** + verb stem + **-en**: **fahr**en *to drive* → **ge**fahr**en** *driven*. Sometimes there is a vowel change in the stem: **sprech**en *to speak* → **ge**spr**o**ch**en** *spoken*.

- Verbs with an inseparable prefix* or infinitives ending in **-ieren** omit the **ge-** prefix: **besuch**en *to visit* → **besuch**t *visited*; **reparier**en *to repair* → **reparier**t *repaired*.

- In verbs with a separable prefix*, the **ge-** is placed between the prefix and the stem: <u>auf</u>machen → **auf**ge**macht**; <u>los</u>fahren → **los**ge**fahren**.

*For more on verbs with prefixes, see Lesson 15.

1 Complete each sentence with the correct past participle from the following regular verbs.

hören   **suchen**   **packen**   **duschen**   **kaufen**

a. Er hat überall .... , aber er findet seine Uhr nicht.

b. Ich habe ein neues Auto ....

c. Hast du schon deinen Koffer ....

d. Habt ihr gebadet? – Nein, wir haben ....

e. Ich habe es im Radio ....

2 Give the past participle or the infinitive of the following irregular verbs.

a. sehen → ....

b. trinken → ....

c. finden → ....

d. laufen → ....

e. nehmen → ....

f. gesprungen → ....

g. geholfen → ....

h. gegessen → ....

i. geblieben → ....

j. gegangen → ....

3 Give the past participle of the following verbs.

a. telefonieren → ....

b. <u>ab</u>schicken* → ....

c. <u>ein</u>laden* → ....

d. <u>an</u>kommen* → ....

e. versuchen → ....

f. gehören → ....

g. verbieten → ....

h. reparieren → ....

*separable prefix

Which auxiliary verb: *haben* or *sein*?

- In perfect tenses, the auxiliary verb **haben** *to have* is used with transitive verbs (those that take a direct object), verbs with a reflexive pronoun and verbs indicating a position, state or lasting condition (with the exception of **bleiben** *to stay, remain* and **sein** *to be*, which take **sein** as the auxiliary):

  Sie haben die Tür geöffnet. *They have opened the door.* (from **öffnen** *to open*)
  Ich habe mich geirrt. *I was wrong.* (from the reflexive **sich irren** *to be mistaken*)
  Wie lange hast du geschlafen? *How long have you slept?* (from **schlafen** *to sleep*)

  Note that **anfangen / beginnen** *to begin, start* and **aufhören** *to stop* are considered verbs that indicate a condition, and thus conjugate with **haben** in perfect tenses.

- The auxiliary verb **sein** *to be* is used with verbs that indicate movement or express a change of condition or location. It is also used with **bleiben**, **sein** and **werden**.

  Ich bin nach Hause gegangen. *I have gone back home.* (from **gehen** *to go*)
  Er ist gewachsen. *He has grown.* (from **wachsen** *to grow*)
  Ich bin in Rom gewesen. *I have been in Rome.* (from **sein** *to be*)

- There are a few rare verbs of movement, e.g. **fahren**, that take either **haben** or **sein** depending on whether they are used transitively or intransitively.

  Ich habe das Auto in die Garage gefahren. *I drove the car into the garage.* (trans.)
  Ich bin nach Berlin gefahren. *I travelled to Berlin.* (intransitive)

4 Complete the sentences with the correct form of *haben* or *sein.* ••

a. Ich .... einen schönen Film gesehen.

b. Wir .... zu Fuß gegangen.

c. Sie (*formal*) .... eine Stunde auf den Bus gewartet.

d. Wie lange .... ihr geblieben?

e. Schnell, der Film .... schon angefangen.

f. Es .... den ganzen Tag geregnet.

5 Rewrite these sentences using the present perfect. ••

a. Er trinkt viel.

→ ....

b. Er läuft schnell.

→ ....

c. Er wäscht sich.

→ ....

d. Es schneit.

→ ....

e. Er ist bei mir.

→ ....

f. Er kommt.

→ ....

Negation

There are two main ways to make a statement negative in German.

- The adverb **nicht** is used to negate a verb, a pronoun, an adverb, an adjective or a noun preceded by a definite article or possessive adjective. Its position depends on the other elements in the sentence. It follows:

  - the finite verb: **Ich esse nicht.** *I'm not eating.*
  - nouns or pronouns used as objects: **Ich glaube es nicht.** *I don't believe it.*
  - specific adverbs of time: **Ich komme morgen nicht.** *I'm not coming tomorrow.*

  It precedes most other kinds of elements, for example:

  - a preposition + object: **Peter wohnt nicht in Bonn.** *Peter doesn't live in Bonn.*
  - a qualifying predicative adjective or adverb: **Sie ist nicht groß**. *She isn't tall.* **Es ist nicht viel.** *It isn't much.*
  - a specific element to be negated (in this case, the sentence often contains **sondern**): **Nicht Peter lebt in Frankreich, sondern sein Bruder.** *It's not Peter who lives in France, but his brother.*

- The negative article **kein** *not a, not any* is used to negate a noun that in an affirmative sentence would be preceded by **ein** or no article at all: **Hier gibt es kein Kino.** *There isn't a cinema here.* **Ich habe keinen Hund.** *I don't have a dog.* **Ich habe keine Zeit.** *I have no time.* Unlike **ein**, it has a plural form: **Es gibt keine Kinos.** (It declines like **ein/mein**: see the declension table on p. 120.)

  Note also the expression **Einmal ist keinmal.** *Just this once.* ('One time is no time.')

6 Make these sentences negative.

a. Ich habe ein neues Auto.

→ ....

b. Sie ist zu schnell gefahren.

→ ....

c. Ich habe Arbeit.

→ ....

d. Ich liebe dich.

→ ....

e. Das ist Gold.

→ ....

f. Ich denke an die Arbeit.

→ ....

7 Connect each sentence with its translation.

1. Ich habe keine Angst. •

2. Ich habe keinen Durst. •

3. Ich habe kein Geld. •

4. Ich habe keine Ahnung. •

5. Ich habe keinen Bock. •

6. Ich habe keinen Hunger. •

7. Ich habe keine Lust. •

• **a.** I have no idea.

• **b.** I'm not hungry.

• **c.** I don't feel like it.

• **d.** I don't fancy it.

• **e.** I'm not thirsty.

• **f.** I don't have any money.

• **g.** I'm not afraid.

Identifying and introducing yourself

Two types of personal identity documents are **der Personalausweis** *identity card* and **der Reisepass** *passport*. The terms used on these documents are useful to know in case you need to fill out any forms. The exercises that follow are a chance to review these.

And do you know this expression? **Sag mir, wer deine Freunde sind, und ich sage dir, wer du bist.** *Tell me who your friends are, and I'll tell you who you are.*

8 Complete the text using these past participles.

studiert geboren gewesen kennen gelernt

gelernt gemacht (x2) gegeben gegangen

Ich heiße Robert Schmitt und bin Deutscher. Ich bin am 5.09.1982 in Köln

.... 2001 habe ich das Abitur .... und bin dann

für 2 Jahre nach Südamerika .... Es war sehr interessant. Ich habe

Spanisch und Portugiesisch ...., und um Geld zu verdienen habe

ich Englisch- und Deutschkurse .... Fremdsprachen interessieren mich

sehr, da ich gern reise. Insgesamt bin ich schon in 54 Ländern

.... Nach meiner Rückkehr aus Südamerika

habe ich von 2003 bis 2010 Medizin an der Universität Berlin

.... und habe dann ein Praktikum im Stadtkrankenhaus

von Heidelberg .... Da habe ich meine Frau ....

Nun arbeite ich als Kinderarzt in einer Klinik in Köln (…).

9 Use the information in the text above to fill in this form,
crossing out what doesn't apply.

1. Name: 2. Vorname:

3. Geburtstag: 4. Geburtsort:

5. Staatsangehörigkeit:

6. Familienstand: ledig, verheiratet, geschieden, verwitwet.

7. Ausbildung/Studium:

8. Beruf:

9. Sprachen:

10. Hobbys:

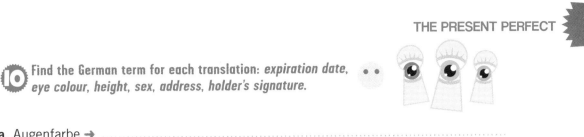

10 Find the German term for each translation: *expiration date, eye colour, height, sex, address, holder's signature.*

a. Augenfarbe ➜ ....

b. Geschlecht ➜ ....

c. gültig bis ➜ ....

d. Wohnort ➜ ....

e. Unterschrift des Inhabers ➜ ....

f. Größe ➜ ....

11 Find the German terms for these hobbies in the puzzle:

music   *drawing/painting*   *sport*

cooking   *cinema*   *dancing*

chess

singing

reading

T	M	A	L	E	N	P	S
U	U	T	O	A	O	F	P
K	S	A	K	S	T	G	O
M	I	N	O	H	E	V	R
B	K	Z	C	I	S	E	T
V	U	E	H	U	A	S	E
O	K	N	E	K	L	A	R
I	S	I	N	G	E	N	U
H	C	E	R	I	S	U	T
R	H	H	S	M	E	I	D
E	A	N	K	I	N	O	D
B	C	M	V	L	H	O	S
B	H	L	M	K	U	L	V

Prima! You've reached the end of Lesson 3. Count up the icons for each exercise and record your results here and in the table on page 128.

4
The simple past

The simple past (or preterite)

- This tense is used to refer to a fully completed event in the past, corresponding to the English simple past (**Es war einmal...** *Once upon a time there was...*). However, today it is more common in formal (i.e. published) writing, whereas the present perfect is usually used in conversational contexts.

- Here are the conjugation endings for regular (weak) verbs: **spielen** *to play* → **ich spielte, du spieltest, er/sie/es spielte, wir spielten, ihr spieltet, sie/Sie spielten**.

- Irregular (strong) verbs take a vowel change in the stem and omit the **-te** in the conjugation endings. This means that the first- and third-person singular have no ending: **sehen** *to see* → **ich sah, du sahst, er/sie/es sah, wir sahen, ihr saht, sie/Sie sahen**; **laufen** *to run* → **ich lief, du liefst, er/sie/es lief, wir liefen**, etc.

- Note that there are a few verbs that differ slightly from these rules, including the very common **sein**, **haben** and **werden**.

1 Complete the table with the simple past forms of *bauen* and *sagen*.

ich	du	er/sie/es	wir	ihr	sie/Sie
baute					
			sagten		

2 Complete the table with the simple past forms of *laufen* and *lügen*.

ich	du	er/sie/es	wir	ihr	sie/Sie
			liefen		
					logen

Complete the tables with the correct verb forms.

Infinitive	Simple past
....	ich trug
....	ich half
....	ich schrieb
....	ich gab

Infinitive	Simple past
nehmen	ich ....
gehen	ich ....
lesen	ich ....
fliegen	ich ....

 Complete the table with the correct simple past forms.

ich	du	er/sie/es	wir	ihr	sie/Sie
war	....	....	....	wart	....
....	....	hatte	hatten	....	....
wurde	....	....	....	....	wurden

Some spelling and pronunciation tips

- Regular (weak) infinitives with a verb stem ending in -d, -t or -n take an -e before the simple past ending to make pronunciation easier: **arbeiten** *to work* → **ich arbeitete, du arbeitetest, er/sie/es arbeitete, wir arbeiteten, ihr arbeitetet, sie/Sie arbeiteten; öffnen** *to open* → **öffnete, öffnetest**, etc.

- Irregular (strong) infinitives with a verb stem ending in -d or -t insert an -e before the ending in the second-person singular and plural to make the pronunciation easier. However, the rule is less strict in the singular: **reiten** *to ride* → **ich ritt, du ritt(e)st, er/sie/es ritt, wir ritten, ihr rittet, sie/Sie ritten.**

- Strong infinitives with a verb stem ending in -s, -ss or -ß take only a -t in the second-person singular: **blasen** *to blow* → **du bliest** (you may also come across the variant **du bliesest**, although this is less frequently used today.

 Conjugate the following verbs in the simple past in the person indicated.

a. ich fand → ihr ....

c. ich las → du ....

b. ich zeichnete → du ....

d. ich redete → sie *(they)* ....

21

6 Derive the infinitive from these nouns and then translate them: *to feel/sense, to ask for/request, to pray, to quarrel, to advise, to land.*

a. die Landung → .... → ....

b. das Gebet → .... → ....

c. der Rat → .... → ....

d. der Streit → .... → ....

e. die Bitte → .... → ....

f. die Empfindung → .... → ....

Special cases

Certain verbs are 'mixed', i.e. a combination of weak and strong conjugations. These mixed verbs are regular in the present tense, but in the simple past they take a stem vowel change like strong verbs while taking the simple past endings of weak verbs: **rennen** *to run* → **r̲ann**te, **r̲ann**test, etc., past participle: **gerannt**.

There are 6 mixed verbs (**brennen, bringen, denken, kennen, nennen, rennen**) and 2 others that can be conjugated as either weak or mixed verbs: **senden** *to send* → **send̲ete** or **s̲and**te, **gesendet** or **gesandt** and **wenden** *to turn* → **wend̲ete** or **w̲and**te, **gewendet** or **gewandt**.

7 Complete these sentences with *rennen, nennen, brennen, kennen* or *denken* in the present tense.

a. Seit wie vielen Jahren .... ihr euch?

b. Hilfe! Es ....

c. Ich heiße Alexander aber alle .... mich Alex.

d. Er .... sehr schnell.

e. Ich .... die ganze Zeit an dich.

S.O.S

8 Give the third-person singular simple past and past participle of these verbs.

a. brennen → .... → ....

b. bringen → .... → ....

c. denken → .... → ....

d. kennen → .... → ....

e. nennen → .... → ....

Saying 'when'

Germans love precision, and the case of which 'when' to use when is a good example of this. Depending on the context, **als**, **wenn** or **wann** is required.

- **als** with a simple past verb conveys a one-off event in the past, of either long or short duration.
  → **Er rief an, als ich im Garten war.** *He phoned when I was in the garden.*

- **wenn** with a simple past verb conveys the sense of *each time,* i.e. *whenever.* It can be preceded by the expression **jedes Mal** *every time.*
  → **(Jedes Mal) Wenn er Zeit hatte, ging er zu Fuß.**
  Whenever he had the time, he went on foot.

- **wenn** with a present tense verb can convey either a one-time or repeated event in the future or a repeated action in the present.
  → **Wenn ich groß bin...** *When I grow up...*
  → **(Jedes Mal) Wenn er kann...** *Whenever he can...*

Note that **wenn** can also mean *if* (see Lesson 6).

- **wann** *When?* is used in questions (including indirect questions).
  → **Wann kommt er?** *When is he coming?*
  → **Ich frage mich, wann er kommt.** *I wonder when he's coming.*

9 Complete these sentences with *als, wenn* or *wann*.

a. .... ich 18 werde, mache ich eine große Feier.

b. Meistens ging ich zu Fuß zur Schule, aber .... es regnete, nahm ich immer den Bus.

c. Ich weiß nicht, ... der Film beginnt.

d. .... er seine erste Stelle bekam, war er 22.

10 Translate these clauses introduced by *als*. They all indicate a one-off event in life.

a. Als er geboren ist*, ...

b. Als er 20 wurde, ...

c. Als er das Abitur machte, ...
  ....

d. Als er heiratete, ...

e. Als er sein erstes Kind bekam, ...
  ....

f. Als er starb, ...

*In this case, the verb is in the passive voice.

Asking and giving the time

- To ask the time, there are two options: **Wie spät ist es?** ('How late is it?') or **Wie viel Uhr ist es?** ('How much clock is it?').

- When giving a specific hour: **Es ist ein Uhr.** *It's one o'clock.* Otherwise, the minutes are stated first and then the hour. Until half past, **nach** *after* is used to give the minutes after the hour: **5:10 → zehn nach fünf** *ten past five*. From half to, **vor** *before* is used to give the minutes to the hour: **5:50 → zehn vor sechs** *ten to six*. The term for 15 minutes is **Viertel** *quarter* and **halb** is *half*. <u>However</u>, be careful with **halb**, because it refers to the hour to come rather than the hour that has passed: **7:30 → halb acht** ('half eight') NOT ~~halb sieben~~.

- Also note that the terms **Mittag** *midday, noon* and **Mitternacht** *midnight* are used only for the specific hour. Otherwise, the number **12** is used: **12:15 → Viertel nach zwölf** *quarter after twelve* NOT ~~Viertel nach Mittag~~ or ~~Mitternacht~~.

- In official timetables (e.g. for trains, buses, planes, etc.), the 24-hour clock is used, so don't be surprised if you see an hour between 13 and 23! In this case, the hour comes first and then the minutes: **13.10 → dreizehn Uhr zehn** (1:10 pm).

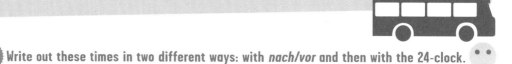

Write out these times in two different ways: with *nach/vor* and then with the 24-clock.

a. 5:45 → .... / ....

b. 8:10 → .... / ....

c. 14:30 → .... / ....

d. 17:15 → .... / ....

e. 8:05 → .... / ....

f. 15:10 → .... / ....

 Circle the correct response.

a. at 10 o'clock → **um/im/am 10 Uhr**

b. around 10:00 → **um/gegen/Richtung 10 Uhr**

c. in the early morning → **am/im/bei Morgen**

d. in the late morning → **am/im/zum Vormittag**

e. at noon → **am/in der/im Mittag**

f. in the afternoon → **am/in der/im Nachmittag**

g. in the evening → **am/im/zum Abend**

h. at night → **durch die/an der/in der Nacht**

i. At what time? → **Um welche Uhr?/Um wie viel Uhr?/An wie viel Uhr?**

Yesterday, today, tomorrow

To talk about a time of day, the construction is **gestern, heute, morgen**, etc. **+ Morgen** (until 10 am), **Vormittag** (10–12 am), **Mittag**, etc. Often, this is similar to the English: **gestern Abend** *yesterday evening*, **morgen Mittag** *tomorrow at noon*, apart from when talking about something on the same day. In German, it's **heute Nachmittag** *this afternoon* ('today afternoon'), **heute Nacht** *tonight* ('today night'), etc. Note also that *tomorrow morning* is **morgen früh** NOT ~~morgen Morgen~~!

13 Translate these time phrases.

a. this evening → ....

c. yesterday morning → ....

b. tomorrow afternoon → ....

d. this afternoon → ....

14 Translate the following words to fill in the crossword.

↓ Down

2J time
6C to wake
6J sleep
9C to ring
11A clock/watch
11E minute
14A to wake up
(formed from the stem of the adjective *awake*)

→ Across

1L to fall asleep
(formed from the stem of *to sleep*)
4E awake
6C alarm clock
6J hour (60 minutes)
8H second

	1	2	3	4	5	6	7	8	9	10	11	12	13	14
A														A
B														
C						W			K					
D														W
E														A
F														
G									G					
H														
I														
J						S								
K														
L	E		N											
M														
N														
O						F								

Great work! You've reached the end of Lesson 4. Now count up the icons for each exercise and record your results here and in the table on page 128.

The future

Talking about the future

- As we've seen, usually the present tense is used to refer to the future in German. Frequently (but not systematically) a time word or phrase is included to indicate that the action will take place in the future: **Am Sonntag machen wir einen Ausflug.** *On Sunday, we will take ('we make') a trip.* **Das mache ich.** *I will do it. ('I do it.')*

- There is also a future tense in German (two in fact: Future I and Future II, but the latter is used very rarely). The simple future (Future I) is a compound tense formed with the auxiliary verb **werden** (conjugated in the present tense) + infinitive. The infinitive goes to the end of the sentence: **Wir werden einen Ausflug machen.** *We will take a trip.* Its use often conveys a supposition regarding a future action or situation: **Es wird wohl regnen.** *It will probably rain.*

- Here are the present tense conjugations of **werden → ich werde, du wirst, er/sie/es wird, wir werden, ihr werdet, sie/Sie werden**.

- As well as an auxiliary verb, **werden** is an independent verb meaning *to become, to begin to be, to get, to turn*, etc. In this case it is often followed by a noun or an adjective: **Sie wurde Ärztin.** *She became a doctor.* **Es wird kalt.** *It's getting cold.*

1 Conjugate these phrases in the simple future.

a. nach Berlin fliegen *(second-person singular)* → ....

b. dir helfen *(first-person plural)* → ....

c. anrufen *(third-person singular, m.)* → ....

d. einen Brief bekommen *(third-person plural)* → ....

2 Rewrite the sentences as in the example.
E.g. Wir werden einen Ausflug machen. → Morgen machen wir einen Ausflug.

a. Sie wird dir eine Mail schreiben. → Morgen ....

b. Das werden sie machen. → Am Dienstag ....

c. Es wird schneien. → Am Wochenende ....

3 Complete the sentences with the following words.

Elektriker   dunkel   **Zeit**   spät   **gelb**   hell

a. Im Sommer wird es um 6 Uhr .... und um 22 Uhr ....

b. Mein Sohn macht eine Lehre *(apprenticeship/training)*. Er wird ....

c. Wir müssen nach Hause. Es wird ....

d. Seit sechs Monaten macht er nichts. Es wird ...., dass er Arbeit sucht.

e. Im Herbst werden die Blätter ....

Before and after

There are different words for *before* and *after* depending on the context.

- **vor** *before, in front of* and **nach** *after* are prepositions (they are followed by the dative case).
  → **Kommst du vor oder nach der Schule?** *Are you coming before or after school?*

- **davor** *before* and **danach** *after, afterwards* are adverbs (note that there are also other adverbs with the same meaning).
  → **Die Schule beginnt um 9 Uhr. Kommst du davor oder danach?**
  School starts at 9 o'clock. Are you coming before or after?

- **bevor** *before* and **nachdem** *after* are subordinating conjunctions and so must be used with a conjugated verb, never with an infinitive!
  → **Ich komme, bevor ich in die Schule gehe.** *I'm coming before I go to school.*

Note the tense agreement in sentences constructed with **nachdem**:

→ Ich <u>komme</u>, nachdem ich die Kinder in die Schule <u>gebracht habe</u>.
   present   present perfect

→ Ich <u>kam</u>, nachdem ich die Kinder in die Schule <u>gebracht hatte</u>.
  simple past   past perfect*

*The past perfect is formed in the same way as the present perfect except that the auxiliary verb is conjugated in the simple past.

4 Find and correct the sentences which are wrong.

a. Bevor dem Essen gehe ich ins Schwimmbad.

→ ....

b. Ich komme, **nachdem** ich die Einkäufe gemacht habe.

→ ....

c. Wenn der Film bis 22 Uhr dauert, gehe ich lieber **vor** etwas essen.

→ ....

d. Essen wir **vor** oder **nachdem** dem Film?

→ ....

5 Conjugate the verbs in parentheses in the correct tenses.

a. Ich rufe dich an, nachdem ich alles .... **(machen)**.

b. Nachdem er lange in Chile .... **(leben)**, kam er zurück.

c. Er .... **(gehen)** nach Deutschland, nachdem er seine Arbeit verloren hatte.

d. Ich .... **(putzen)** die Küche, nachdem du den Kuchen gebacken hast.

Saying what you do

When it comes to professions, remember that no article is used in German when saying what you do: **Ich bin Koch.** *I'm a cook* (m.). The general rule for forming the feminine is to add the suffix **-in: der Lehrer, die Lehrerin** *teacher*. Sometimes an accent is added to the vowel: **der Koch, die Köchin**. There are a few exceptions, such as **der Krankenpfleger, die Krankenschwester** *nurse*. Some professions have only one form for both the masculine and feminine.

6 Find the German term for each of these professions (all masculine):
policeman, nurse, doctor, lawyer, hairdresser, gardener, fireman, actor, craftsman, computer scientist, mechanic, insurance agent.

a. Handwerker → ....

b. Polizist → ....

c. Rechtsanwalt → ....

d. Informatiker → ....

e. Feuerwehrmann → ....

f. Gärtner → ....

g. Schauspieler → ....

h. Mechaniker → ....

i. Arzt → ....

j. Krankenpfleger → ....

k. Friseur → ....

l. Versicherer → ....

7 Give the professions related to these verbs in the feminine.
E.g. fischen → die Fischerin

a. kochen → ....

b. singen → ....

c. musizieren → ....

d. backen → ....

e. verkaufen → ....

f. tanzen → ....

g. lehren → ....

h. putzen → ....

8 List the professions (from exercises 6 and 7, masculine and feminine) practiced in these locations. There may be more than one.

a. Krankenhaus → ....

b. Schule → ....

c. Orchester → ....

d. Restaurant → ....

e. Werkstatt → ....

f. Kanzlei → ....

g. Praxis → ....

h. Geschäft → ....

i. Bäckerei → ....

j. Meer → ....

'Tomorrow' or 'morning'

In German, these two words are homonyms: **morgen** *tomorrow* and **der Morgen** *morning* (before 10 am). They are found in several German expressions.

9 Use the literal translations to try to find equivalent English expressions or else explain what they mean.

a. Morgen ist auch noch ein Tag. ('Tomorrow is also still a day.')

→ ....

b. Morgen, morgen, nur nicht heute, sprechen immer faule Leute.
('Tomorrow, tomorrow, only not today, speak always lazy people.')

→ ....

c. Morgenstund hat Gold im Mund. ('Morning hour has gold in the mouth.')

→ ....

Super! You've completed Lesson 5. Now count up the icons for each exercise and record your result here and in the table on page 128.

6
The subjunctive II

The subjunctive II

- There are two subjunctive moods in German: subjunctive I is used essentially when writing reported speech, and subjunctive II is used to express a supposition or possibility, corresponding to the conditional in English.

- The present subjunctive II is used to convey something hypothetical or conditional in the present or future. There are two ways it can be formed.

  - Compound form: **werden** (in the present subjunctive II) + infinitive, which goes to the end of the clause: **Wir würden es anders machen.** *We would do it differently.*

  - Simple form: the endings **-e**, **-est**, **-e**, **-en**, **-et**, **-en** are added to the past tense stem. If the stem vowel is **a**, **o** or **u**, it takes an umlaut (except **wollen** and **sollen**).

Infinitive	Simple past stem	Present subjunctive II	
haben	ich hatt	ich hätt + e	hätte
wollen	du wollt	du wollt + est	wolltest

In everyday speech, the compound form is much more common, but the simple form is required for **sein**, **haben**, **werden**, the 6 modal verbs and **wissen**. Note that in the second-person singular and plural present subjunctive II of **sein**, the **e** can be omitted: **du wärst / ihr wärt** instead of **du wärest / ihr wäret** (less common).

- The past subjunctive II is used to express something contrary-to-fact, i.e. that did not happen in the past. It is formed with **haben** or **sein** (in the present subjunctive II) + past participle, which goes to the end of the clause: **Ich hätte es gemacht.** / *would have done it.* **Ich wäre mitgefahren.** *I would have driven with [you].*

 Conjugate these verbs in the present subjunctive II using the compound form.

a. schlafen – ich

→ ....

b. lernen – er

→ ....

c. gehen – ihr

→ ....

d. anrufen – du

→ ....

e. lesen – wir

→ ....

f. warten – Sie

→ ....

2 Conjugate these verbs in the present subjunctive II using the simple form.

a. wissen – wir

➔ ....

b. können – du

➔ ....

c. wollen – ihr

➔ ....

d. sein – sie *(they)*

➔ ....

e. dürfen – du

➔ ....

f. müssen – er

➔ ....

g. wissen – ihr

➔ ....

h. sein – ich

➔ ....

i. haben – Sie

➔ ....

3 Conjugate these verbs in the past subjunctive II.

a. kommen – ich

➔ ....

b. bleiben – wir

➔ ....

c. sagen – du

➔ ....

d. fragen – ihr

➔ ....

e. schreiben – er

➔ ....

f. gehen – Sie

➔ ....

Conditional 'if' sentences

There are three types of conditional sentence, each with its own tense sequence.

- If the condition is possible, both the main clause and the **wenn** *if* subordinate clause are in the present tense:
  - ➔ **Wenn ich kann, komme ich mit euch.** *If I can, I'll come* ('I come') *with you.*

- If the condition is an imaginary situation in the present, both the main clause and the **wenn** *if* subordinate clause are in the present subjunctive II:
  - ➔ **Wenn ich könnte, würde ich mit euch kommen.** *If I were able to* ('If I could'), *I would come with you.*

- If the condition is an imaginary situation in the past (i.e. something that is contrary-to-fact because it did not actually happen), both the main clause and the **wenn** *if* subordinate clause are in the past subjunctive II:
  - ➔ **Wenn ich gekonnt hätte, wäre ich mit euch gekommen.** *If I could have* (or *if I had been able to*), *I would have come with you.*

(For more on word order, see Lesson 13.)

And finally, a useful conditional expression: **Wenn das Wörtchen wenn nicht wär, wär mein Vater Millionär.** ('If the word 'if' didn't exist, my father would be a millionaire.') *If wishes were horses, beggars would ride.*

4 Conjugate the verbs in the conditional clause using the appropriate tense.

a. Wenn ich Geld .... **(haben)**, würde ich eine Weltreise machen.

b. Wenn wir jünger .... **(sein)**, hätten wir es gemacht.

c. Wenn du Glück .... **(haben)**, kannst du einen Computer gewinnen.

d. Wenn es nicht .... **(regnen)**, wären wir ans Meer gefahren.

e. Ich würde dich heiraten, wenn ich .... **(können)**.

f. Ich wäre der glücklichste Mann der Welt, wenn du mich .... **(lieben)**.

5 Connect each *wenn* (if) exclamation to its English equivalent.

1. Wenn ich das gewusst hätte! •
2. Wenn ich nur mehr Geld hätte! •
3. Wenn Sie nichts dagegen haben! •
4. Wenn es möglich wäre! •
5. Wenn es so ist! •

• **a.** If it were possible!
• **b.** If you have nothing against it!
• **c.** If it's like that!
• **d.** If I had known that!
• **e.** If only I had more money!

If or whether?

In some contexts, *if* and *whether* are used interchangeably in English. However, in German, their usage doesn't overlap.

• **wenn** *if* expresses a condition.

• **ob** *whether* is used in indirect questions or to present alternative choices, so often comes after verbs such as **sich fragen, nicht sicher sein, nicht wissen, wissen** (in a question). It is always preceded by a comma. **Ich frage mich, ob er kommt.** *I wonder* ('ask myself') *if he's coming.*

6 *Wenn* or *ob*? Have a go!

a. Ich bin mir nicht sicher, ... er kommt.

b. .... du möchtest, können wir ihn einladen.

c. Wissen Sie, ... es noch weit ist?

d. Wir wären früher gefahren, ... ich das Auto gehabt hätte.

e. .... es morgen schön wird, das frage ich mich.

f. Frag doch, ... er mit dem Zug oder mit dem Auto kommt.

g. Ich weiß nicht, ... eer zufrieden gewesen wäre, ... ich ihm dieses Buch geschenkt hätte.

Homonyms

Certain nouns have the same (or almost the same) form in the singular, but are differentiated by gender, e.g. **der See** *lake* and **die See** *sea*. Most have different plural forms, though there are some exceptions, such as **die Seen** *lakes* or *seas*. Usually, one of the homonyms is common in everyday language, whereas the other tends to be a more specialized term. Here are a few examples.

7 In these pairs of homonyms, connect each word to its translation.

1. der Band / die Bände •   • **a**. volume *(book)*
2. das Band / die Bänder •   • **b**. ribbon

3. der Kaffee / die Kaffeesorten •   • **c**. coffee
4. das Café / die Cafés •   • **d**. café

5. der Leiter / die Leiter •   • **e**. ladder
6. die Leiter / die Leitern •   • **f**. leader

7. die Steuer / die Steuern •   • **g**. tax
8. das Steuer / die Steuer •   • **h**. steering wheel / rudder

9. die Taube / die Tauben •   • **i**. deaf man
10. der Taube / die Tauben •   • **j**. pigeon

11. der Junge / die Jungen •   • **k**. young *(animals)*
12. das Junge / die Jungen •   • **l**. boy

13. der Tor / die Toren •   • **m**. gate / goal
14. das Tor / die Tore •   • **n**. fool

Clothing vocabulary

If you decide to do some clothes shopping, a word of warning: international clothes sizes vary! To convert women's clothing sizes, add 28 to the UK size or 30 to the US size; for men's clothing (US and UK), add 10. Just to be sure, don't hesitate to ask for **die Umkleidekabine** *the fitting room.*

8 Fill in the missing vowels in these clothes.

a. **H _ S _** (f. sing.) *trousers*

b. **H _ MD** (n.) *shirt*

c. **R _ CK** (m.) *skirt*

d. **M _ NT _ L** (m.) *coat*

e. **KL _ _ D** (n.) *dress*

f. **J _ CK _** (f.) *jacket*

g. **P _ LL _** (m.) *pullover, sweater*

h. **SCH _ H _** (m. pl.) *shoes*

i. **H _ T** (m.) *hat*

j. **_ N T _ RH _ S _** (f. sing.) *underpants, underwear*

k. **STR _ MPF _** (m. pl.) *socks, stockings*

l. **STR _ MPFH _ S _** (f. sing.) *tights*

9 Use these words to complete the sentences.

groß   Größe   Farbe   passt   lang
anprobieren   kurz   klein   Paar

a. Welche .... haben Sie? *What size do you wear?*

b. In welcher ....? *In what colour?*

c. Kann ich es bitte ....? *May I please try it on?*

d. Es ist zu .... und zu .... *It's too small and too short.*

e. Es ist zu .... und zu .... *It's too big and too long.*

f. Ich nehme dieses .... Schuhe.
  I'll take this pair of shoes.

g. Das .... mir. *That fits/suits me.*

Translate these colours to fill in the crossword.

↓ Down

2A pink
5C white
6G green
7B orange
9G blue
12F brown

→ Across

1A grey
2C black
6G yellow
9H purple
12G red

	1	2	3	4	5	6	7	8	9	10	11	12	13	14
A														
B														
C														
D														
E														
F														
G														
H														
I														
J														

II Connect the two halves of the following accessories. Then give their translation: *umbrella, sunglasses, handkerchief, handbag, braces/suspenders, belt, wallet.*

a. Hand • • schirm → ....

b. Gür • • träger → ....

c. Hosen • • beutel → ....

d. Geld • • tuch → ....

e. Taschen • • tasche → ....

f. Regen • • brille → ....

g. Sonnen • • tel → ....

Great! You've completed Lesson 6. It's time to count up the icons for the exercises and record your result here and in the table on page 128.

7

The passive voice

The passive voice

In the passive, the subject of the sentence receives the action rather than performing it. This puts the emphasis on the receiver of the action. German has two passives.

- The passive describing an action or process is formed with **werden** + past participle. This passive often corresponds to a progressive/continuous form in English.
  - Present: **Die Katze isst die Maus. → Die Maus wird von der Katze gegessen.**
  The cat eats the mouse. → The mouse is being eaten by the cat.
  - Simple past: **Die Katze aß die Maus. → Die Maus wurde von der Katze gegessen.**
  The cat ate the mouse. → The mouse was being eaten by the cat.

If the processual passive is used in a perfect tense, note that **werden** forms perfect tenses with **sein**, and in the passive voice the past participle is **worden** (no ge-).

- The passive describing a finished state or result is formed with **sein** + past participle. It is used mainly in the present and the simple past.
  Das Brot ist/war gebacken. *The bread is/was baked.*

Be careful: although the statal (or **sein**) passive looks like the English passive, the meaning can be different. The statal passive always describes a <u>result or finished state</u>, whereas the processual (or **werden**) passive describes an <u>action</u>:
Das Brot wird gebacken. *The bread is being baked.* (action/process)
Das Brot ist gebacken. *The bread is baked.* (description of a state)

The **sein** passive is much less common than the **werden** passive.

I Change these sentences from the passive to the active voice or vice versa.

a. Der Gärtner hat den Rasen gemäht.

→ ....

b. Die Techniker kontrollieren oft die Maschinen.

→ ....

c. Die Sekretärin schrieb den Brief.

→ ....

d. Dieses Bild wurde 1906 von Picasso gemalt.

→ ....

e. Von wem wurde die Zauberflöte komponiert?

→ ....

f. Ich bin von einer Wespe gestochen worden.

→ ....

g. Die Kinder packen die Geschenke ein.

→ ....

h. Das Haus wurde von meinem Vater gebaut.

→ ....

2 Rewrite these sentences in the statal *(sein)* passive. ●●

E.g. Um fünf Uhr wird der Kuchen gebacken. → Um sieben Uhr ist der Kuchen gebacken.

a. Um 20 Uhr wird das Geschäft geschlossen.

→ Um 21 Uhr ....

b. Um 12 Uhr wird das Essen gekocht.

→ Um 13 Uhr ....

c. Am Morgen wurde alles vorbereitet.

→ Am Abend ....

d. Vor der Feier wurde das ganze Haus geputzt.

→ Für die Feier ....

The impersonal passive

In some passive sentences, the agent of the action doesn't need to be specified: **Das Haus wird restauriert.** *The house is being restored.* This is called the impersonal passive. If no words precede the verb in this construction, a time or place phrase or **es** can be added as a 'dummy subject': **Es wird viel gearbeitet.** *A lot of work is being done.* It is also quite common to make an impersonal sentence active by using **man** one: **Man arbeitet viel.** ('One works a lot.'). In English, we often use 'they' or 'people' in this context: **Man arbeitet von 9-17 Uhr.** *They work from 9:00 to 5:00.*

3 Change these sentences to the impersonal passive. ●●

a. Man hat das Auto repariert.

→ ....

b. Man tanzt viel.

→ ....

c. Man renoviert die Fassade.

→ ....

d. Damals schrieb man Briefe.

→ ....

e. Im Sommer aß man später.

→ ....

f. Man hat mich zum Essen eingeladen.

→ ....

4 Circle the correct past participle. ●●

a. Das Auto wurde von der Polizei wieder **empfunden** • **erfunden** • **gefunden**. *(found)*

b. Wir wurden sehr nett **gefangen** • **empfangen** • **angefangen**. *(welcomed)*

c. Das Essen ist schon **aufgestellt** • **bestellt** • **ausgestellt**. *(ordered)*

d. Ich bin von der Polizei **angehalten** • **behalten** • **gehalten** worden. *(stopped)*

e. Der Kranke wurde gründlich **versucht** • **untersucht** • **gesucht**. *(examined)*

f. Ich werde ständig **zerbrochen** • **gebrochen** • **unterbrochen**. *(interrupted)*

To see, to look, to watch

As in English, there are different verbs for this: **sehen** *to see* is a strong verb (simple past: **ich sah**, past participle: **gesehen**) and **schauen** *to look (at)* is a weak verb (simple past: **ich schaute**, past participle: **geschaut**). Different nuances of meaning are conveyed by using these verbs with various words (adverbs, prepositions, reflexive pronouns, prefixes, etc.). Here are some of the possible constructions.

- **gut/schlecht sehen** *to see well/badly*: **Ich sehe schlecht.** *I see badly.*

- **jemanden/etwas sehen** *to see someone/something*: **Ich habe sie noch nie gesehen.** *I've never seen her before.* **Siehst du den Vogel?** *Do you see the bird?*

- **schauen** + prepositional phrase: *to look through, towards, etc.*: **Warum schaust du ständig zum Fenster hinaus?** *Why do you keep looking out of the window?*

- **jemanden/etwas ansehen** or **anschauen** *to look at someone/something*: **Er sah/schaute mich böse an.** *He looked at me angrily. / He gave me a nasty look.*

- **sich etwas ansehen** or **anschauen** *to look at something with attention or interest*: **Hast du dir die Fotos angesehen/angeschaut?** *Have you looked at the photos?*

- Note than while **ansehen** is used in many contexts to mean *to watch*, including to watch a film, the term for *to watch television* is **fernsehen**: **Wir sehen heute fern.** *We're watching TV today.*

5 Circle the correct word(s) to complete each sentence.

a. Er hat mich lächelnd **gesehen** • **zugeschaut** • **angeschaut** • **angeseht**.

   He looked at me with a smile.

b. Er hat sich dein Bild lange **gesehen** • **angesehen** • **geschaut** • **angeschaut**.

   He took a long look at your drawing.

c. Ich möchte mir die Kirche **ansehen** • **anschauen** • **zusehen** • **schauen**.

   I would like to see the church.

d. Ohne Brille kann ich nichts **ansehen** • **sehen** • **anschauen**.

   Without glasses, I can't see anything.

e. Sie hat mehrmals auf die Uhr **gesehen** • **geschaut** • **angeschaut** • **geseht**.

   She looked at her watch several times.

Food vocabulary

Let's review some vocabulary related to meals: **das Frühstück** ('early piece') *breakfast*, **das Mittagessen** ('midday meal') *lunch* and **das Abendessen** ('evening meal') or **das Abendbrot** ('evening bread') *dinner*. The latter term comes from the tradition in Germanic countries of eating a light evening meal consisting mainly of bread with cold cuts and cheese between 6 and 7 pm. This tradition is less widespread than it used to be, as many people today eat a light lunch and have their main hot meal at dinner.

6 Use the following words to complete the sentences.

Gemüse   Nachspeise   Trinkgeld   Getränke

Kuchen   Fleisch   Obstsalat   Rechnung

a. Sie haben ein Menü mit einer Vorspeise, Hauptspeise und ....

b. Als Hauptspeise können Sie entweder Fisch oder .... nehmen, und als Beilage haben Sie die Wahl zwischen Kartoffeln, Reis oder ....

c. Dazu bestellen Sie auch .... : Wein, Bier oder Wasser.

d. Haben Sie sonst noch einen Wunsch? Ein Eis, ein Stück .... oder, wenn Sie auf Ihre Linie achten wollen, einen leichten ....

e. Zum Schluss fragen Sie nach einem Kaffee mit der .... Und normalerweise geben Sie der Bedienung auch ....

7 Connect each word to its translation.

1. Biergarten •   • **a.** beer festival

2. Bierkrug •   • **b.** beer garden

3. Bierkeller •   • **c.** beer barrel

4. Bierfass •   • **d.** beer mug

5. Bierfest •   • **e.** beer cellar

8 Guess the following fruits and vegetables.

A vegetable that starts with:

→ K (9 letters) – needed to make fish and chips: ....

→ K (7 letters) – orange in colour and shares the same first three letters as the word above: ....

→ S (5 letters) – green and is eaten raw, usually with dressing: ....

→ B (5 letters) – comes in different colours (green, white or brown) and can grow in strings or pods: ....

→ G (6 letters) – German word for vegetables: ....

A fruit that starts with:

→ A (5 letters) – pressed to make juice or cider: ....

→ T (6 letters) – red and not often considered a fruit as it isn't sweet: ....

→ O (6 letters) – same name as its colour: ....

→ E (9 letters in the plural) – red forest fruit whose four vowels are all **e**: ....

→ F (7 letters in the plural) / O (4 letters) – both these words mean 'fruit' in German: .... / ....

9 Complete the words in this exchange.

– Ich würde gern einen _ _ **s** _ _ reservieren. Für heute Abend 4 _ _ _ **s** _ _ _ _.

– Ja gern. Für wie viel **U** _ _?

– 20 **U** _ _ auf den _ _ _ _ **n** von Robert Schmitt. Wäre es draußen auf der **T** _ **r** _ _ _ _ _ möglich?

– Ich schaue mal, ob noch etwas **f** _ _ _ ist. (...) Nein, um die Uhrzeit sind wir leider schon **v** _ _ _. Aber ab 21 **U** _ _ wäre es möglich.

– Nein, danke. Dann nehmen wir lieber einen **T** _ _ _ _ **d** _ **i** _ _ _ _.

– In Ordnung. Wie war der **N** _ _ _?

– Robert Schmitt.

Fill in the crossword.

↓ Down

2F glass

5C spoon

9A serviette, napkin

→ Across

9A salt

2C plate

4F pepper

1H fork

8I knife

	1	2	3	4	5	6	7	8	9	10	11	12	13
A													
B													
C													
D													
E													
F													
G													
H													
I													

Expressing feelings

Many verbs expressing feelings are reflexive in German (e.g. **sich ärgern** *to be angry*, **sich freuen** *to be glad*, **sich wundern** *to be surprised*, etc.). Remember that reflexive verbs always conjugate with a pronoun to indicate that the subject is acting upon itself. (See the declension table on p. 121 for the different forms of reflexive pronouns.) Here are some German expressions to say how you feel.

Connect each expression to its translation.

1. Das regt mich auf.   •
2. Das beruhigt mich.   •
3. Das ist mir egal.   •
4. Das macht mich rasend / verrückt.   •
5. Das macht mich krank.   •
6. Das haut mich um.   •

• **a**. *That's reassuring.*
• **b**. *It doesn't matter to me.*
• **c**. *That makes me angry/crazy.*
• **d**. *That upsets/annoys me.*
• **e**. *That floors me.*
• **f**. *That makes me sick.*

Toll! You've reached the end of Lesson 7. It's time to count up the icons for the exercises and record your result here and in the table on page 128.

8

Nouns & the nominative

The nominative

This case is used for the subject of the sentence and certain words that modify it. If the word answers the question **Wer** *Who?* or **Was?** *What?* and is the subject of the verb, it should be in the nominative. Nominative declensions mainly affect articles, pronouns, possessives, demonstratives (see declension tables, pp. 120–121) and adjectives used before nouns. Apart from case, declensions depend on the gender and number of a noun. Note that the nominative plural definite article is always **die**.

> Wer **kommt aus Berlin?** → Der **neue Direktor** (m.) / Die **neue Direktorin** (f.).
> Was **ist für die Kinder?** → Das **Buch** (n.) **ist für die Kinder.**
> Wer **sind diese Kinder?** → Sie sind die **Söhne** (pl.) / die **Töchter** (pl.) **von Sabine.**

Nouns

To choose the right declension, you first need to know the gender of the noun the word refers to. Here are a few pointers to help with some everyday terms.

- Masculine: males (**der Mann** *man, husband*) (except for diminutives), most of the days of the week (**der Dienstag** *Tuesday*), parts of the day (**der Nachmittag** *afternoon*), months (**der Juli** *July*), seasons (**der Herbst** *autumn*) and points of the compass (**der Süden** *south*), most nouns derived from verbs (**der Schlaf** *sleep*), and many nouns ending in **-er** , **-ler**, **-ismus**, **-or**, **-ig** or **-ling** (**der Motor** *engine*).

- Feminine: females (**die Frau** *woman, wife*) (except for diminutives), most names of trees (**die Eiche** *oak*), flowers (**die Tulpe** *tulip*), fruits (**die Zitrone** *lemon*), numbers (**die Vier** *four*), and nouns ending in **-ei, -in, -ion, -heit, -keit, -ung, -ur** or **-schaft** (**die Freiheit** *freedom*, **die Freundschaft** *friendship*).

- Neuter: the very young (**das Kind** *child, baby*), most metals (**das Silber** *silver*), letters of the alphabet (**das A**), colours (**das Rot** *red*), languages (**das Spanisch**), verbs used as nouns (**das Essen** *eating, meal*), collective nouns with the prefix **Ge-** (**das Gebirge** *mountain range*), diminutives ending in **-chen** or **-lein** (**das Fräulein** *young lady*), and many nouns ending in **-um, -ium** or **-ment** (**das Datum** *date*).

I Complete these words with the nominative declensions.

a. Dies...... klein...... Junge möchte dich etwas fragen.

b. Das ist ein....... schön...... Instrument.

c. Dies..... alt..... Dame ist 98 Jahre alt.

d. Weiß........ Schuhe passen besser zu deinem Kleid.

e. Dies....... jung....... Mann wartet schon seit einer Stunde.

2 Identify the nominative noun in each sentence, then phrase the corresponding questions using *wer* or *was*.

E.g. Die Kinder sind angekommen. → die Kinder → Wer ist angekommen?

a. Das Paket ist für Paul. → .... → ....

b. Paul sucht den Hausschlüssel. → .... → ....

c. Hier liegt der Ausweis. → .... → ....

d. Sie ist die neue Deutschlehrerin. → .... → ....

.... / ....

3 Give the gender of these nouns.

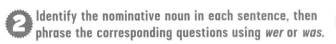

a. .... Mutter	**i**. .... Schmetterling
b. .... Freundin	**j**. .... Morgen
c. .... Leben	**k**. .... Baby
d. .... Zeitung	**l**. .... Birne
e. .... Gold	**m**. .... Zwanzig
f. .... Mittwoch	**n**. .... M
g. .... Gemüse	**o**. .... Arabisch
h. .... Rose	**p**. .... Grün

4 Give the other gender of each term.
E.g. der Mann → die Frau

a. der Lehrer → .... | **e**. die Verkäuferin → ....

b. die Freundin → .... | **f**. die Ärztin → ....

c. der Junge → .... | **g**. der Bauer → ....

d. der Vater → .... | **h**. der Bruder → ....

Forming the plural

Unfortunately, there are various ways that nouns form the plural in German. Although there are exceptions, in general, most plurals follow these rules:

- no ending (but an umlaut is added if the vowel in the noun is **a**, **o**, **u**) for most masculine and neuter nouns ending in **-er**, **-en**, **-el**, **-chen** or **-lein**: **das Messer → die Messer**; **der Vater → die Väter**. This rule also applies to two feminine nouns: **die Mutter → die Mütter**; **die Tochter → die Töchter**.

- **-e** ending (and sometimes an umlaut on **a**, **o**, **u**) for many masculine nouns and some neuter and one-syllable feminine nouns: **der Monat → die Monate**; **die Bank → die Bänke**.

- **-er** ending (and sometimes an umlaut on **a**, **o**, **u**) for many neuter and some masculine nouns: **das Kind → die Kinder**; **der Wald → die Wälder**.

- **-n** or **-en** ending for numerous feminine and a few neuter nouns: **die Tafel → die Tafeln**; **das Auge → die Augen**.

- **-nen** ending for feminine nouns ending in **-in**: **die Lehrerin → die Lehrerinnen**.

- **-se** ending for neuter and feminine nouns ending in **-nis**: **das Geheimnis → die Geheimnisse**.

- **-s** ending for nouns ending in **-a**, **-i**, **-o** and for many foreign nouns: **das Auto → die Autos**.

Be careful: certain nouns that are homonyms in the singular have different plural forms: **der Strauß** *bouquet* **→ die Sträuße**; **der Strauß** *ostrich* **→ die Strauße**.

 **5** Give the plural of the following nouns.

a. der Wagen

→ ....

b. die Blume

→ ....

c. die Sängerin

→ ....

d. das Foto

→ ....

e. der Stuhl

→ ....

f. der Vogel

→ ....

 6 Put these words in the singular.

a. die Bücher → das ....

b. die Früchte → die ....

c. die Tische → der ....

d. die Götter → der ....

e. die Hefte → das ....

f. die Büros → das ....

In these pairs of homonyms, connect each noun to its translation. You should be able to deduce unknown terms as at least one of the words in each pair is everyday vocabulary.

1. die Bank / die Bänke •   • a. bench
2. die Bank / die Banken •   • b. bank

3. der Mann / die Männer •   • c. vassal
4. der Mann / die Mannen •   • d. man

5. der Rat / die Räte •   • e. councillor
6. der Rat / die Ratschläge •   • f. advice

7. der Stock / die Stockwerke •   • g. stick/baton
8. der Stock / die Stöcke •   • h. floor/storey

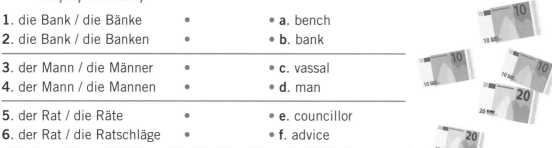

Compound nouns

German is famous for its ability to construct long compound words, using smaller words as building blocks. Some of these words, for example, high numbers, have up to 60 letters, and the record to date is held by a word composed of 90 letters – too long to include here! Compound nouns may be composed entirely of nouns or of a verb + noun or adjective + noun. The gender is determined by the final component in the word, known as the 'primary word': **der Grundschullehrer** *primary school teacher* (because **der Lehrer** is masc.).

8 **List the final component (primary word) and its gender.**

a. Großonkel → ....

b. Kindermädchen → ....

c. Deutschübung → ....

d. Abendessen → ....

e. Musikinstrument → ....

f. Blumenstrauß → ....

g. Wochentag → ....

h. Haupteingang → ....

9 Turn the below into compound nouns by adding the following primary words.

-schirm   -hose   -brand   -kreme   -tuch   -stich

-urlaub   -anzug   -nacht   -kleid   -meister   -sprossen

a. der Bade ....

b. der Bade ....

c. die Bade ....

d. das Bade ....

e. der Sommer ....

f. die Sommer ....

g. die Sommer .... *(freckles)*

h. das Sommer ....

i. der Sonnen .... *(sunstroke)*

j. der Sonnen ....

k. die Sonnen ....

l. der Sonnen ....

Talking about where you live

Some types of homes: **das Haus** *house*, **das Einfamilienhaus** *detached house*, **das Doppelhaus** *semi-detached house*, **das Reihenhaus** *terraced house(s)*, **das Apartment** *apartment*.

10 Underline the primary word in these nouns and connect each to its translation. [Not all are compound words.]

1. die Eingangstür •   • **a**. children's room

2. die Küche •   • **b**. bathroom

3. das Schlafzimmer •   • **c**. living room

4. das Badezimmer •   • **d**. entrance/front door

5. das Wohnzimmer •   • **e**. dining room

6. das Esszimmer •   • **f**. bedroom

7. der Briefkasten •   • **g**. letterbox/mailbox

8. das Kinderzimmer •   • **h**. kitchen

11 Complete the compound nouns with one of the following primary words and translate them. [Not all can be turned into compound words.]

-bett   -maschine   -regal   -schrank   -tisch

a. der Ess ....

b. der Schreib ....

c. das Kinder ....

d. der Kleider ....

e. der Stuhl ....

f. die Couch ....

g. der Sessel ....

h. die Spül ....

i. die Wasch ....

j. der Kühl ....

k. das Bett ....

l. das Bücher ....

12 Fill in the missing letters.

a. Jemand hat an die Tür **ge _ l _ _ ft**. *Someone has knocked at the door.*

b. Es hat **gek_ _ ng _ lt**. *The doorbell rang. ('It has been rung.')*

c. Kannst du bitte die Tür **a _ f _ ac _ _ n**? *Can you open the door, please?*

d. Komm bitte **h _ _ e _ n**! *Please come in!*

e. Nimm bitte **P _ _ _ z**! *Please take a seat!*

f. Darf ich dir etwas zum Trinken **a _ b _ _ t _ n**? *May I offer you something to drink?*

g. Danke für deinen **_ es _ _ h**. *Thank you for your visit.*

13 Find these terms in German in the puzzle.

bathtub   sink

mirror shower

toilets

(2 words, one of which is colloquial)

W	N	M	K	O	U	J	I	S
A	S	K	M	C	A	V	K	P
S	X	L	L	T	S	X	O	I
C	T	O	I	L	E	T	T	E
H	C	R	K	L	H	W	N	G
B	A	D	E	W	A	N	N	E
E	Z	U	D	F	E	E	B	L
C	L	S	S	X	C	X	A	P
K	L	C	A	F	K	D	A	M
E	H	H	Y	O	E	F	E	J
N	N	E	I	U	N	O	D	B
R	D	V	P	G	R	U	C	V

14 Find these terms in German in the lines of letters.

house number

house key

telephone number

address (2 synonyms)

postal code

caretaker

H A U S N U M M E R P O S T
L E I T Z A H L H A U S M E I S
T E R A D R E S S E T E L E F
O N N U M M E R H A U S S C H
L Ü S S E L A N S C H R I F T

Excellent! You've completed Lesson 8. It's time to count up the icons for the exercises and record your result here and in the table on page 128.

9

The accusative

The accusative

This case is used for the direct object in a sentence and certain words that modify it. If the word answers **Wen?** *Who?* or **Was?** *What?* and receives the action of the verb, it should be in the accusative. (See the declension tables, pp. 120–121.) It is used:

- to mark a direct object: e.g. in **jemanden/etwas** sehen *to see someone/something*. In the accusative, the feminine, neuter and plural share the same forms as the nominative case; only the masculine singular changes.
  Wen hast du gesehen?
  → **Ich habe den Sohn** (m.) / **die Tochter** (f.) **von Paul gesehen.**
  Was hast du gesehen?
  → **Ich habe einen französischen Film** (m.) / **ein schönes Theaterstück** (n.) **gesehen.**

  So the accusative is required in these common formulations: **jemanden fragen** *to ask someone* (**Ich habe dich gefragt.** *I have asked you.*), **jemanden/etwas brauchen** *to need someone/something* (**Ich brauche den Saft.** *I need the juice.*). In some contexts a double accusative is required: **jemanden etwas kosten** *to cost someone something* (**Es kostet mich eine Million.** *It costs me a million.*)

- after certain prepositions, such as: **durch** *through, by*, **für** *for*, **gegen** *against*, **ohne** *without*, **um** *around*: **Wir fahren ohne dich.** *We're travelling without you.* Note that certain prepositions form contractions with **das**: **durch das → durchs; für das → fürs; um das → ums.**

- in time phrases using **letzt-** *last*, **dies-** *this*, **nächst-** *next*, article + **ganz-** *all the, the whole*: **Wir waren letzten Dienstag bei ihm.** *We were with him last Tuesday.* **Wir waren den ganzen Tag bei ihm.** *We were with him the entire day.*

- after the expression **es gibt** *there is/are*: **Wo gibt es hier einen Supermarkt?** *Where is there a supermarket?*

1 Replace the definite article with the correct declension of the demonstrative adjective *dies-*.

a. den jungen Schauspieler → ....

b. das neue Theaterstück → ....

c. die russische Tänzerin → ....

d. die französischen Filme → ....

2 Complete the sentences with these nominative phrases, changing the declension if necessary.

a. Kannst du bitte .... beim Bäcker kaufen?

b. Viele Lehrer sind gegen ....

c. Heute haben wir .... geschrieben.

d. Geh nicht ins Kino! Das ist ....

e. Es gibt .... im Zentrum.

f. Hier kommt .... mit deinem Päckchen.

die neue Schulreform

der Briefträger

ein kleiner Test

ein kleines Hotel

frische Brötchen

kein schöner Film

3 Complete these sentences with the correct personal pronouns.
E.g. Das Buch ist gut. Kauf es.

a. Hier sind die Papiere. Bitte, nimm .... !

b. Hast du den Wagen zur Reparatur gebracht? – Ja, ich habe .... gestern gebracht.

c. Habt ihr morgen Zeit? Wir möchten .... zum Essen einladen.

d. Du sprichst zu schnell. Ich verstehe .... nicht.

Indefinite pronouns

The indefinite pronouns **einer, eine, ein(e)s** *one, someone* and **keiner, keine, kein(e)s** *none, not any, not anyone* decline like **der, die, das**. The indefinite pronoun **ein-** has no plural form, but the negative plural form is **keine** (see table, p. 121). In the neuter singular, the **e** can be omitted – both forms are possible.

Haben Sie Kinder?
– Ja, ich habe **ein(e)s**. (= ein Kind)
– Nein, ich habe **keine**. (= keine Kinder)

Ich möchte einen Apfel.
– Ich möchte auch **einen**. (= einen Apfel)
– Ich möchte **keinen**. (= keinen Apfel)

4 Complete the sentences with the correct indefinite pronoun in the nominative or the accusative.

a. Hast du eine Idee? – Nein, ich habe ....

b. Er hat ein Auto. – Ich habe auch ....

c. Ist das ein Porsche? – Nein, das ist ....

d. Gibt es im Hotel ein Schwimmbad? – Ja, es gibt ....

5 Add the missing endings. The gender is given in parentheses for certain words.

a. Meine Schwester heiratet dies............. Samstag.

b. Er war d............. ganz............. Woche *(f.)* verreist.

c. Nächst............. Monat *(m.)* wird es besser.

d. Er war ein............. ganz............. Jahr *(n.)* weg.

e. Letzt............. Mal *(n.)* konnte ich nicht kommen.

A lot, many, much, very

The words **viel** *much, a lot* (or the plural **viele** *many*) and **sehr** *very* are extremely frequently used, so they are **sehr nützlich** *very useful* to master!

- When **viel** is used before an uncountable noun in the singular, it doesn't take an ending: **Er hat viel Arbeit.** *He has a lot of work.* But when it comes before a plural countable noun, it has to decline: **Er hat viele Freunde.** *He has many friends.*

- Used with a verb, **viel** is an adverb and does not change form. It expresses the idea of quantity: **Er isst viel.** *He eats a lot.*

Note that **viel** can be used with **sehr** to convey an even greater amount or intensity: **Sehr vielen Dank!** *Very many thanks!* **Er isst sehr viel.** *He eats a great deal.*

- When **sehr** is used with an adjective or adverb it means *very*: **Es ist sehr warm.** *It's very warm.* **Sehr gern!** *With pleasure!* ('Very gladly!')

- When used with a verb, **sehr** means *a lot, very much, really, greatly*: **Es ärgert mich sehr, dass er nicht kommen kann.** *It really annoys me that he can't come.* **Ich vermisse dich sehr.** *I miss you a lot.*

6 Complete the sentences with either *viel(-)* or *sehr.*

a. Ich habe nicht .... Zeit.

b. Ich freue mich .... , dass du kommst.

c. .... Leute sind gekommen.

d. Er schläft ....

e. Er arbeitet mit ....
Ausländern zusammen.

f. Er ist .... traurig.

g. Er schläft .... lange.

7 Translate the following sentences.

a. You *(informal sing.)* drink a lot. → ....

b. He drinks a lot of water. → ....

c. There are many people. → ....

d. He loves you *(informal sing.)* very much. → ....

e. It's very beautiful. → ....

f. She has a great deal of money. → ....

8 Translate these expressions.

a. Viel Spaß! → ....

b. Viel Erfolg! → ....

c. Viel Glück! → ....

d. Viel Vergnügen! → ....

e. Vielen Dank! → ....

f. Sehr gern! → ....

g. Sehr geehrter Herr... → ....

9 Connect each sentence to its translation.

1. Es ärgert mich sehr.   •   • **a**. It really hurts. *(physical or emotional)*

2. Es wundert mich sehr. •   • **b**. It weighs on me greatly. *(worries me)*

3. Es freut mich sehr.   •   • **c**. It really annoys me.

4. Es tut mir sehr weh.   •   • **d**. It helps me very much.

5. Es belastet mich sehr. •   • **e**. It surprises me a lot.

6. Es hilft mir sehr.   •   • **f**. It pleases me a great deal.

Measurements and descriptions

der (Kilo)Meter	(K)m
das (Kilo)Gramm	(K)g
das Pfund	500 Gr.
Stundenkilometer	Km/h

alt	old
groß	big/tall
weit	far
tief	deep
breit	wide

wert	worth
hoch	high
schnell	fast
schwer	heavy
lang	long

In many cases, the construction for giving measurements or descriptions is similar to English, but the accusative case is required after **sein: Wie tief ist das Becken?** *How deep is the basin?* **Das Becken ist einen Meter tief.** *The basin is one metre deep.* If the context is clear, sometimes the answer can simply be a number: **Wie groß bist du?** *How tall are you?* **Ich bin eins siebzig.** *I am 1 [m] 70 [cm].* **Wie alt bist du?** *How old are you?* **Ich bin zwanzig.** *I am 20.* To give a weight, **wiegen** *to weigh* is often used: **Wie viel wiegst du?** *How much do you weigh?* But to say how much something weighs, you say it is 'x kilos heavy'!

10 Complete the sentences with the correct adjective.

a. Das Baby ist erst einen Monat ....

b. Der Tisch ist einen Meter achtzig .... und achtzig cm ....

c. Es ist ein Kilo ....

d. Der Eiffelturm ist dreihundertvierundzwanzig Meter ....

e. Das Dorf ist nur einen Kilometer .... von hier.

11 Complete the questions with the correct adjective.

a. *How wide ...?* → Wie ....?

b. *How long ...?* → Wie ....?

c. *How old ...?* → Wie ....?

d. *How fast ...?* → Wie ....?

e. *How heavy ...?* → Wie ....?

f. *How big ...?* → Wie ....?

12 Put the letters in the correct order to find these words in German.

a. weight → E / W / H / T / I / G / C → das ....

b. age → R / L / T / E / A → das ....

c. speed → K / T / I / E / E / G / G / I / D / H / C / S / N / I / W → die ....

d. height → Ö / H / H / E → die ....

e. length → Ä / N / G / L / E → die ....

13 Translate these question words to fill in the crossword. If there are two words, leave an empty box between them.

↓ Down

3K *how many* (2 words)

4G *who* (nominative)

5C close synonym of **warum**

6I *whom* (accusative)

8E close synonym of **wieso**

10C *what*

13A *where to*

→ Across

4D *how*

8E *whose*

4G *where from*

6I *whom* (dative)

3K *when*

1M *how long* (2 words)

2P *how many times* (2 words)

	1	2	3	4	5	6	7	8	9	10	11	12	13
A													
B													
C													
D													
E													
F													
G													
H													
I													
J													
K													
L													
M													
N													
O													
P													
Q													
R													

Das ist es! You've finished Lesson 9. It's time to count up the icons for the exercises and record your results here and in the table on page 128.

10

The dative

The dative

This case is used for the indirect object in a sentence. If the word answers **Wem?** *To whom?* the action of the verb is directed, it should be in the dative. It is used:

- to mark an indirect object: for example, in <u>**jemandem**</u> schreiben *to write <u>to someone</u>*, 'someone' is an indirect object. **Wem** hast du geschrieben? → **Dem** Sohn (m.) **von Paul und der Tochter** (f.) **von Peter.**

  Another example is <u>**jemandem**</u> zuhören *to listen <u>to someone</u>* (**Hörst du** mir **zu?** *Are you listening <u>to me</u>?*) Note that some verbs take the dative case when the English equivalent would be a direct object, e.g. **jemandem danken** *to thank someone*, **jemandem folgen** *to follow someone*, **jemandem gratulieren** *to congratulate someone*, **jemandem helfen** *to help someone*, **jemandem widersprechen** *to contradict someone* and **jemandem zuschauen** *to watch someone*.

- after certain prepositions, such as: **aus** *out of, outside, from,* **bei** *at, with, near,* **mit** *with,* **nach** *after, to,* **seit** *since,* **von** *from, of, by,* **zu** *to, at, on the occasion of*: **Ich gehe** zum **Arzt.** *I'm going <u>to the doctor</u>.* **Ich bin** beim **Arzt.** *I'm <u>at the doctor's</u>.*

  Note that certain prepositions form contractions with **dem** and **der**: **bei dem → beim, in dem → im, von dem → vom, zu dem → zum** and **zu der → zur.**

In the dative, plural nouns add an **-n** (except nouns that already end in **-n** or **-s**): **die Tische** *tables* (nom.) → **den Tischen** (dat.).

I Add the appropriate declensions (for certain words, the gender is given in parentheses).

a. Sie kommt aus ein............. klein............. Stadt *(f)*.

b. Hast du d............. Kinder............. *(pl.)* die neue Kamera gezeigt?

c. Hast du d............. Bruder von Sabine geschrieben?

d. Die Tasche gehört dies............. Dame da.

e. Ich habe ein............. alt............. Mann geholfen, den Koffer zu tragen.

f. Hör dies............. Mann zu!

g. Er ist seit ein............. Monat *(m.)* krank.

2 Complete these sentences with the correct dative personal pronoun.

a. Sag .... **(ich)** bitte, wann du kommst!

b. Gib .... **(sie,** *f. sing.***)** alles!

c. Ich schicke .... **(Sie)** alles per Mail.

d. Ich gratuliere .... **(du)** zum Geburtstag.

e. Kannst du .... **(wir)** bitte helfen?

3 Replace the definite article with the correct indefinite article.

a. der einzigen Schülerin → ....

b. den kleinen Kindern → ....

c. dem armen Mann → ....

d. der alten Dame → ....

4 Connect each sentence to its translation. (Note that in English the usage of objects and tenses is sometimes different.)

1. Ich befehle es dir. •

2. Ich biete es dir an. •

3. Ich empfehle es dir. •

4. Ich leihe es dir. •

5. Ich verbiete es dir. •

6. Ich schwöre es dir. •

• **a.** I forbid you to do it.

• **b.** I'll lend it to you.

• **c.** I order you to do it.

• **d.** I swear to you.

• **e.** I recommend it to you.

• **f.** I'm offering it to you.

Word order

In German, the position of direct (accusative) and indirect (dative) objects in a sentence varies depending on whether they are personal pronouns or nouns:

- with two nouns, the <u>indirect object</u> comes before the direct object:
  Ich diktiere <u>der Sekretärin</u> den Brief. *I'm dictating a letter <u>to the secretary</u>.*

- with two personal pronouns, the direct object comes before the <u>indirect object</u>:
  Ich diktiere ihn <u>ihr</u>. *I'm dictating it <u>to her</u>.*

- with a pronoun and a noun, the pronoun always comes first, regardless if it is indirect or direct: **Ich diktiere <u>ihr</u> den Brief.** *I'm dictating a letter <u>to her</u>.*

5 Complete these sentences in the correct word order.

a. Ich habe .... geschickt. **(euch / ein Päckchen)**

b. Ich schenke .... **(dir / die Uhr)**

c. Ich habe .... gesagt. **(es / ihr)**

d. Ich habe .... gegeben. **(das Geld / deinem Bruder)**

6 Rewrite these sentences, replacing the underlined objects with a pronoun and observing the correct word order.

a. Ich habe <u>Ana</u> eine Mail geschrieben. → ....

b. Ich habe Paul <u>die Mail</u> geschrieben. → ....

c. Wir schenken <u>meinen Eltern</u> <u>das Buch</u>. → ....

'Not much' and 'too much'

- When **wenig** *little, few, not much, not many* is used before an uncountable noun in the singular, it generally doesn't take an ending: **Er hat wenig Zeit.** *He has little time.* In the plural, it often declines, but this is optional: **Er hat wenige Freunde.** *He has few friends.* (See declension type II, p. 120.)

- Used with a verb, **wenig** does not change form: **Er isst wenig.** *He eats little.*

In both cases, **wenig** can be preceded by **zu** to mean *too little/few*: **Er hat zu wenig Zeit.** *He has too little time.* **Er isst zu wenig.** *He eats too little.* (Note that in English, it is often more common to express *little/few* with *not much/many* and a negative verb: *He doesn't eat much. He doesn't have many friends.*)

- When **zu viel** *too much/many* is used before a noun it only declines in the plural (see p. 50): **Es gibt zu viele Leute.** *There are too many people.*

- **zu viel** can also be used with a verb:
  Sie hat zu viel gegessen. *She has eaten too much.*

- To convey intensity rather than quantity, **zu sehr** can be used with a verb:
  Es belastet mich zu sehr. *It bothers me too much.*

- **zu** with an adjective or an adverb simply means *too*: **Es ist zu warm.** *It's too warm.*

7 Translate the following sentences.

a. He has too much work. ➜ ....

b. It's too far. ➜ ....

c. I don't see her much. ➜ ....

d. He sleeps too little. ➜ ....

e. He annoys me too much. ➜ ....

f. He practices too little sport. ➜ ....

The dative in impersonal expressions

German has a number of frequently used impersonal expressions (i.e. in which the subject is left unspecified) that require a pronoun in the dative. The best known is no doubt **Wie geht es dir?** ('How goes it for you?') **Mir geht es gut, danke. Und dir?** ('For me goes it well, thanks. And for you?') – note that all these pronouns are in the dative. These constructions can be a bit tricky to get used to. And to complicate things further, sometimes the same verb can take either the accusative or the dative: **Es ekelt mich davor.** or **Es ekelt mir davor.** *It disgusts me.* (from the verb **sich davor ekeln** *to be disgusted by*).

8 Connect each sentence to its translation.

1. Es schmeckt mir.   •

2. Es gefällt mir.   •

3. Mir ist es lieber so.   •

4. Es fällt mir schwer.   •

5. Mir ist schlecht.   •

6. Es passt mir nicht.   •

7. Es kommt mir komisch vor.   •

• **a**. It seems strange to me.

• **b**. I prefer it like that.

• **c**. I feel ill/sick.

• **d**. It tastes good.

• **e**. I like it. / It appeals to me.

• **f**. I find it hard.

• **g**. It doesn't fit/suit me.

Parts of the body

The German expression **Es hat weder Hand noch Fuß.** ('It has neither hand nor foot.') is equivalent to the English *I can't make head nor tail of it.* In both languages, the metaphor is based on parts of the body, but not the same ones. Do you know the words for the parts of the body in German? Let's review them.

9 List the number next to the corresponding body part.

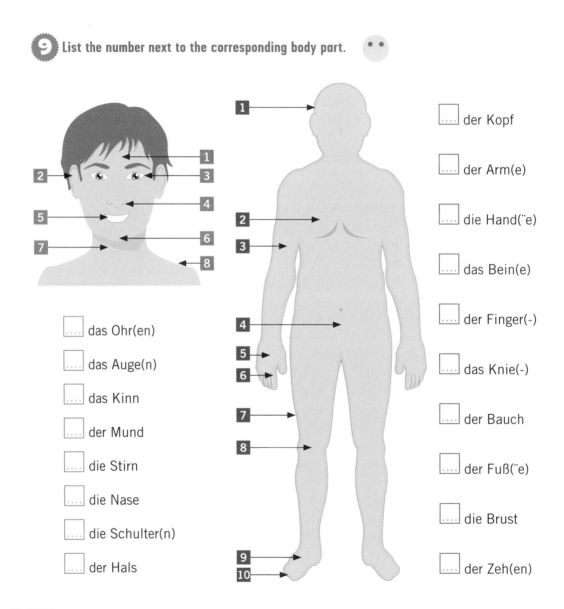

.... das Ohr(en)

.... das Auge(n)

.... das Kinn

.... der Mund

.... die Stirn

.... die Nase

.... die Schulter(n)

.... der Hals

.... der Kopf

.... der Arm(e)

.... die Hand("e)

.... das Bein(e)

.... der Finger(-)

.... das Knie(-)

.... der Bauch

.... der Fuß("e)

.... die Brust

.... der Zeh(en)

10 Translate these words to fill in the crossword.

	1	2	3	4	5	6	7	8	9	10	11	12	13	14
A														
B														
C		S												
D										G				
E				K		A		K						
F														
G														
H		R												
I				U										
J														
K										E				
L														
M														

↓ Down

2C aches / pains

4C (a) cold

6E pharmacy

8A medicine

10D health

13H ill / sick

→ Across

4E illness

1H doctor *(m.)*

9K healthy

11 Here are a few German expressions that refer to body parts. Can you use the literal translations to guess their equivalent in English or else explain what they mean?

a. Halt den Mund! ('Hold the mouth!')

→ ....

b. Ich habe die Nase voll. ('I have the nose full.')

→ ....

c. Er lebt auf großem Fuß. ('He lives on big foot.')

→ ....

d. Lügen haben kurze Beine. ('Lies have short legs.')

→ ....

e. Mach dir keinen Kopf. ('Make you no head.')

→ ....

Klasse! You've reached the end of Lesson 10. It's time to count up the icons for the exercises and record your result here and in the table on page 128.

11
The genitive

The genitive

This case is used to show possession or a close relationship, answering the question **Wessen?** *Whose?* (see the declension tables, pp. 120–121). It is used:

- to link nouns or noun phrases to express possession: **der Lehrer → das Buch des Lehrer**s *the teacher's book* ('the book of the teacher'). In the genitive, masculine and neuter singular nouns add an **-s** or **-es** (apart from weak masculine nouns). A rule of thumb is that if the noun has one syllable (or already ends in **-s**) it takes **-es**: **der Mann → das Buch** des **Mann**es; **das Krankenhaus → die Fläche** des **Krankenhaus**es. Nouns with more than one syllable normally take **-s**.

However, the genitive is falling into disuse in spoken German, and possession is increasingly expressed with the preposition **von** + dative: **das Buch** von dem **Lehrer**.

- after certain prepositions such as **trotz** *despite*, **während** *during* or **wegen/aufgrund** *because of*. But here too, the dative often replaces the genitive in spoken German: **wegen** des **Verkehr**s *due to traffic* → **wegen dem Verkehr**.

- There is also a special genitive used only with proper nouns, called the Saxon genitive. It is essentially the same as the English possessive, but without an apostrophe: **Frau Baumbach**s **Haus**; **Dirk**s **Freund**. In a sentence, the definite article of the 'possessed' noun disappears, so the adjective must decline (see declension type II, p. 120): **Der ältere Bruder von Gisela studiert in Amerika. → Gisela**s **älterer Bruder studiert in Amerika.** *Gisela's older brother studies in America.*

1 Rewrite using the genitive.

a. die Tasche von dem kleinen Mädchen

→ ....

b. das Auto von einem reichen Mann

→ ....

c. die Schulbücher von den neuen Schülern

→ ....

d. der Stock von einer alten Frau

→ ....

2 Rewrite using *von*.

a. die Koffer der deutschen Touristen

→ ....

b. das Fahrrad des kleinen Mädchens

→ ....

c. die Sporthalle der neuen Schule

→ ....

d. der Plan eines alten Flughafens

→ ....

3 Change the sentences with *von* to the Saxon genitive and vice versa.

a. Das Buch von Peter liegt auf dem Tisch.
→ ....

b. Kennst du den neuen Freund von Sabine?
→ ....

c. Pauls kleiner Bruder ist in meiner Klasse.
→ ....

d. Ich habe Richards Frau eine Mail geschrieben.
→ ....

4 Complete the sentences with *trotz*, *während* or *wegen*.

a. .... schlechten Wetters haben wir gebadet.

b. ....des Streiks konnten wir nicht zurückfliegen.

c. Er hat .... des ganzen Konzerts geschlafen.

d. .... eines Unfalls wurde die Autobahn gesperrt.

Weak and mixed masculine nouns

- Some masculine nouns take an **-n** or **-en** ending in all cases except the singular nominative. These are mainly nouns that refer to (male) people or animals. For example, nationalities that end in an **-e** in the masculine singular take **-n** in all other cases and the plural. If a weak masculine noun ends in a consonant, it takes **-en***.

singular: **der Russe, den Russen, dem Russen, des Russen**
plural: **die Russen, die Russen, den Russen, der Russen**
singular: **der Pilot, den Piloten, dem Piloten, des Piloten**
plural: **die Piloten, die Piloten, den Piloten, der Piloten**

Many of these nouns end in **-ist, -ent, -ant**, vowel + **t, -aph, -oph, -ekt, -urg, -sch** or **-e**.

*Exception: **der Herr** takes an **-n** rather than an **-en**, but only in the singular:
singular: **der Herr, den Herrn, dem Herrn, des Herrn**
plural: **die Herren, die Herren, den Herren, der Herren**

- Mixed masculine nouns such as **der Buchstabe** *letter* (of the alphabet), **der Friede** *peace* and **der Name** *name* decline both like weak masculine nouns (by adding **-n**) and strong nouns (by adding **-s** in the genitive singular): **der Name, den Namen, dem Namen, des Namens**; pl. **die Namen, die Namen, den Namen, der Namen**.

5 Complete the table.

Singular	Nominative	der Student	....
	Accusative	....	den Löwen
	Dative	....	....
	Genitive	....	....

6 Complete the table.

Plural	Nominative	die Studenten	....
	Accusative	....	die Löwen
	Dative	....	....
	Genitive	....	....

7 Translate these weak masculine nouns.

a. der Prinz ➜ ....

b. der Mensch ➜ ....

c. der Bär ➜ ....

d. der Polizist ➜ ....

e. der Junge ➜ ....

f. der Affe ➜ ....

g. der Komponist ➜ ....

h. der Rabe ➜ ....

i. der Held ➜ ....

Names of countries

Only a few countries are preceded by an article: for example, **die Türkei** *Turkey*, **die Schweiz** *Switzerland*, **die Vereinigten Staaten / die USA** *the United States* (plural), and **die Niederlande** *the Netherlands* (plural). A few others can be used with or without an article, e.g. **Iran / der Iran**. The majority of country names are neuter.

Different prepositions are used before country names depending on whether the meaning conveys location (**in** *in*), origin (**aus** *from*) or destination (**nach** *to*):
Wo wohnt ihr? ➜ **Paul wohnt in Deutschland und ich wohne in der Schweiz.**
Woher kommt ihr? ➜ **Paul kommt aus Deutschland und ich komme aus der Schweiz.**
Wohin fahrt ihr? ➜ **Paul fährt nach Deutschland und ich fahre in die Schweiz.**

In the last example, note that a different preposition is used in certain contexts with the names of countries without an article and those with an article. The names of towns and of regions follow the same rules.

8 Complete with the appropriate preposition or prepositional phrase.

a. Er fliegt .... USA. **(in die / nach / nach den)**

b. Er war .... Spanien. **(in / nach / aus)**

c. Er fährt .... Italien. **(zu / nach / in das)**

d. Warst du schon einmal .... Rom? **(in / in der / nach)**

Nationalities and languages

- There are two main patterns for forming a nationality from a country name:

  - Most nationalities are strong nouns: to form these, the suffix **-er** is added to the name of the country (for a male inhabitant). Some take an umlaut on the **a**, **o** or **u**. The feminine is formed by adding **-erin**. **Holland → der Holländer, die Holländerin** (pl. **die Holländer, die Holländerinnen**). In some cases, the name of the country is slightly modified. **Amerika → der Amerikaner(-), die Amerikanerin(nen); Spanien → der Spanier(-), die Spanierin(nen)**.

  - Some nationalities are weak nouns: the masculine singular ends in **-e** (in all other cases and the plural, an **-n** is added: see p. 61). The feminine ends in **-in**. Apart from the addition of the suffix, many of the word stems can differ from the name of the country: **China → der Chinese(n), die Chinesin(nen)**.

There is one important exception: **Deutschland → der/die Deutsche** (m./f.), **die Deutschen** (pl.) or **ein Deutscher** (m.), **eine Deutsche** (f.), **Deutsche** (pl.). Unlike other nationalities, this is an adjectival noun, so it declines like an attributive adjective (see declension tables, p. 120).

- The names of languages are adjectival nouns. They end in the suffix **-isch** and when used as nouns are written with a capital letter: **die englische Sprache → Englisch**; (although the following suffix omits the **i**) **die deutsche Sprache → Deutsch**.

9 Give the nationality (masculine) or the name of the country/continent.

a. England → ....
b. der Afrikaner → ....
c. Frankreich → ....
d. der Asiat → ....

e. Europa → ....
f. der Ire → ....
g. Italien → ....
h. der Grieche → ....

10 Name the language for each country.

a. Spanien → ....
b. China → ....
c. England → ....

d. Japan → ....
e. Italien → ....
f. Russland → ....

Great! You've completed Lesson 11. It's time to count up the icons for the exercises and record your result here and in the table on page 128.

12
Two-way prepositions

Two-way prepositions

- Some prepositions can take an object in the accusative or the dative, depending on the context. These are prepositions that refer to either position or location. They are:

an	auf	hinter	in	neben	über	unter	vor	zwischen
at, on, to	at, to, on, upon	behind	in, into	next to, beside, near	above, about across, over	under, below	in front of	between

They take the accusative when they indicate a direction or a change in location: **Ich gehe an die Tafel.** *I go to the blackboard.* They take the dative when they simply indicate location: **Ich bin an der Tafel.** *I am at the blackboard.*

Careful, location does not necessarily imply something static; the dative is also used to express movement within the same place: **Er geht in dem Raum hin und her.** *He's walking back and forth in the room.* (dative) as opposed to **Er geht in den Raum.** *He goes into the room.* (accusative)

Certain prepositions can contract with **das** and **dem**: an + das → ans, an + dem → am, auf + das → aufs, in + das → ins, in + dem → im. They can also contract with other prepositions, although this is less common (e.g. **hinter + dem → hinterm**).

- Although often the equivalent prepositions are used in German and English, there are quite a few cases in which the usage is not the same: **Ich muss schnell ins Büro.** *I have to go to ('in') the office quickly.* **Das Spiel ist im Fernsehen.** *The game is on ('in') television.*

Among the spatial prepositions, **in** is often a bit tricky for English speakers. It is used with words describing a place (e.g. school, swimming pool, cinema, theatre, restaurant, etc.) where English often uses *at*, or an audiovisual context (television, radio, Internet, etc.) where English often uses *on*.

1 Circle the correct answer.

a. Wir gehen **in die/in der** Stadt.

b. Wir wohnen **in die/in der** Stadt.

c. Ich bin **ans/am** Telefon.

d. Jeden Sommer fahren wir **ans/am** Meer.

e. Die Kinder spielen **in den/im** Garten.

f. Er hat **auf die/auf der** Couch geschlafen.

2 Complete with one of the two-way prepositions. ••

a. Setzen Sie sich bitte .... den Tisch!

b. Er ist .... den Kopf gefallen.

c. Gehst du gern .... s Theater? *(s = contracted article)*

d. Kann ich mich .... dich setzen?

e. Hannover liegt .... Hamburg und München.

f. Wir fliegen .... den Wolken.

3 Complete the sentences with these nouns/noun phrases. ••
They all take the preposition *in*.

das Kino   die Schule   die Zeitung   das Schwimmbad   der falsche Bus   das Bett   das Internet

a. Gestern haben wir einen schönen Film .... gesehen.

b. Ich bin müde. Ich gehe ....

c. Er ist sehr sportlich. Jeden Morgen um 7 Uhr geht er ....

d. Morgen wird's schön. Ich habe es .... gelesen.

e. Ich bin .... eingestiegen. Ich sollte die Linie 5 und nicht 6 nehmen.

f. Schau mal ....! Da findest du bestimmt einen Billigflug.

g. Die Kinder sind ....

Verbs indicating 'position' or 'action'

German has several verbs that describe the position of things where we use *to be*, and corresponding verbs to express the action of moving something to a position where we use *to put*. Verbs giving a position take the dative and are intransitive (no direct object). Verbs expressing movement take the accusative and are transitive (a direct object, which is sometimes reflexive: e.g. **sich setzen** *to sit 'oneself' down*).

Dative	Accusative
stehen (stand, gestanden) *to be standing upright*	**stellen (stellte, gestellt)** *to stand something upright*
liegen (lag, gelegen) *to be lying down*	**legen (legte, gelegt)** *to lay something down*
hängen (hing, gehangen) *to be hanging up*	**hängen (hängte, gehängt)** *to hang something up*
sitzen (saß, gesessen) *to be sitting down*	**setzen (setzte, gesetzt)** *to set something down*

4 **Complete the sentences with a verb of position or action.**

a. Ich habe alle Papiere auf deinen Schreibtisch ....

b. Willst du dich nicht lieber auf diesen Stuhl ....?

c. Die Blumen .... auf dem Tisch.

d. Deine Jacke .... in meinem Schrank.

e. Er .... im Bett.

5 **Circle the correct response.**

a. **Häng / stell / hing** bitte den Mantel an den Haken!

b. Ich habe den ganzen Tag **gesitzt / gesessen / gesetzt**.

c. Ich **liege / stelle / stehe** schon seit 40 Minuten an der Bushaltestelle und es kommt kein Bus.

d. Hat jemand von euch meinen Geldbeutel genommen? Er **legte / lag / stand** doch hier.

e. Als ich ankam, **standen / stellten / lagen** alle vor der Haustür, um mich zu begrüßen.

Reflexive pronouns

A reflexive pronoun indicates the same person or thing as the subject (e.g. *myself, yourself, himself, oneself*, etc.). They can occur in the accusative or dative case. The forms differ from the personal pronouns only in the third person, which is always **sich**. Although English has few reflexive verbs, they are much more frequent in German.

Accusative	Dative
ich wasche mich	**ich kaufe** mir **ein Auto**
du wäschst dich	**du kaufst** dir **ein Auto**
er wäscht sich	**er kauft** sich **ein Auto**
wir waschen uns	**wir kaufen** uns **ein Auto**
ihr wascht euch	**ihr kauft** euch **ein Auto**
sie/Sie waschen sich	**sie/Sie kaufen** sich **ein Auto**

6 **Conjugate these verbs in the present tense.**

a. sich kämmen *(second-person sing.)* → ....

b. sich freuen *(third-person sing.)* → ....

c. sich einen Tee machen *(first-person pl.)* → ....

d. sich setzen *(first-person sing.)* → ....

7 Translate the sentences using these reflexive verbs.

sich beeilen · sich vorbereiten · sich benehmen
sich umdrehen · sich anziehen · sich erholen

a. I don't have time; I have to get ready.

→ ....

b. Don't turn around! *(informal sing.)* He's here.

→ ....

c. She behaved very well.

→ ....

d. We rested well during the holidays.

→ ....

e. Hurry up! *(informal sing.)* The film starts in five minutes.

→ ....

f. I'm still not dressed.

→ ....

8 Connect each German verb to its translation.

1. sich ändern •   • **a**. to be afraid

2. spazieren gehen •   • **b**. to go for a walk

3. sich schämen •   • **c**. to drown

4. geschehen •   • **d**. to wake up

5. ertrinken •   • **e**. to happen

6. sich fürchten •   • **f**. to be ashamed

7. aufstehen •   • **g**. to change, to alter

8. aufwachen •   • **h**. to stand/get up

Vocabulary for getting around town

Adverbs of place:

hier	here
da	there
dort	over there
oben	above, up
unten	below, down
rechts	on the right
links	on the left
hinten	at the back
vorn	at the front
drinnen	inside
draußen	outside
drüben	on the other side, across

- To say where you are (location), adverbs are used on their own: **Ich bin unten.** *I'm downstairs.*
- To say where you are coming from (origin), they are preceded by **von**: **Ich komme von unten.** *I'm coming from downstairs.*
- To say where you are going to (destination), they are preceded by **nach**: **Ich gehe nach unten.** *I'm going downstairs.*

Note also the direction particles **her** *here* (movement towards speaker) and **hin** *there* (away from speaker) to express direction (see Lesson 15).

9 Complete the sentences with the adverbs indicated.

a. Ich bin .... *(up here)*

b. .... ist es zu warm. Lasst uns .... gehen. *(inside/outside)*

c. Sitzt du lieber .... oder .... ? *(on the left / on the right)*

d. Er kam .... *(from the right)*

e. Setz dich .... *(at the back)*

10 Complete the sentences below with the correct words.

nehmen

Richtung

verfahren

geradeaus

verlaufen

komme

biegen

a. Wie .... ich zum Bahnhof?
How do I get to the station? ('How do I come...')

b. Fahren Sie immer weiter ....!
Go straight on/ahead!

c. .... Sie nach links ab!
Turn left.

d. .... Sie die zweite Straße rechts!
Take the second street on the right.

e. Sie haben sich .... / ....!
You've gone the wrong way. (walking/driving)

f. Sie müssen in die andere ....!
You must go in the other direction.

Translate the words to fill in the crossword.

<table>
<tr><td colspan="2">↓ Down</td><td colspan="2">→ Across</td></tr>
</table>

↓ Down

1B hospital
3B museum
5B railway station
10I post office
11A church
14B bakery
16I cinema

→ Across

7B swimming pool
3D school
9F theatre
1J pharmacy
10K stadium
1L supermarket

	1	2	3	4	5	6	7	8	9	10	11	12	13	14	15	16
A																
B																
C																
D																
E																
F																
G																
H																
I																
J																
K																
L																

Well done! You've reached the end of Lesson 12. It's time to count up the icons for the exercises and record your result here and in the table on page 128.

Word order

Main clauses

German syntax (i.e. sentence structure) can be rather tricky. Word order varies according to whether a unit in a sentence is a main or subordinate (dependent) clause, as well as according to the position of the units within the sentence. Let's start with the rules for a main clause (a clause that can stand alone as a sentence).

- In the main clause of a statement, the verb is always in the second position. (Note that the first position could be a group of words, so the verb is not always the second word – however, it always comes directly after the introductory element.)
  Peter fährt morgen nach Ulm. / Morgen fährt Peter nach Ulm. / Nach Ulm fährt Peter morgen. (the last example is less frequent) *Peter is travelling to Ulm tomorrow.*

- In a question without a question word, the verb comes first: **Hast du Hunger?**

- The parts of a verb used in a main clause are not found together. The conjugated element is in the second position, but the past participle, separable prefix or infinitive goes to the end of the clause:
  Gestern ist Peter nach Ulm gefahren. *Yesterday Peter went ('has gone') to Ulm.*
  Peter reist morgen nach Ulm ab. *Peter is leaving for Ulm tomorrow.* (**abreisen**)
  Peter möchte morgen nach Ulm fahren. *Peter would like to travel to Ulm tomorrow.*

- In general, an adverb or adverbial phrase giving information about time, manner or place is placed at the beginning of the clause (or if used together, they appear in that order). In a question, the question word comes first:
  Morgen Abend gehen sie nach Ulm. *Tomorrow evening they're going to Ulm.*
  Wer möchte morgen nach Ulm fahren? *Who would like to go to Ulm tomorrow?*

1 Following the example, place the elements of the sentence in the correct order, starting with the subject and then the time word or phrase.

E.g. hat angerufen / gestern / sie / mich → Sie hat mich gestern angerufen. / Gestern hat sie mich angerufen.

a. zieht um / mein Sohn / im Mai

→ .... / ....

b. heute / er / ist losgefahren

→ .... / ....

c. kannst / du / nächste Woche / bei mir wohnen

→ .... / ....

Subordinate clauses

The rules are different for a subordinate clause (a clause that gives extra information about a main clause, but can't stand on its own as a sentence). Note that in German, main and subordinate clauses are always separated by a comma.

- In a subordinate clause, the conjugated verb goes to the very end. (But the other elements follow the same rules for position as in a main clause.)
  Sie weiß nicht, ob Peter morgen nach Ulm fährt. **/ Sie weiß nicht, ob Peter morgen nach Ulm** abreist. **/ Sie weiß nicht, ob Peter morgen nach Ulm** fahren kann. **/ Sie weiß nicht, ob Peter gestern nach Ulm** gefahren ist.

Generally, the subject comes directly after the conjunction, but it may also be placed after an adverb: **Sie weiß nicht, ob morgen Peter nach Ulm fährt.**

- If the subordinate clause starts the sentence, the subject and verb in the main clause switch places. (But the other elements follow the usual rules for position: e.g. the past participle, separable prefix or infinitive is at the end of the clause.)
  Ob Peter morgen nach Ulm fährt, weiß sie **nicht. / Ob Peter morgen nach Ulm fährt,** kann sie **nicht** <u>sagen</u>. **/ Wann Peter morgen nach Ulm fährt,** hat sie **nicht** <u>gesagt</u>. **/ Wenn Peter morgen nach Ulm fährt,** kommt sie **auch** <u>mit</u>.

2 Place the elements of the subordinate clause in the correct order after *Sie weiß nicht, ob…* • •

E.g. den Brief / ihr Freund / hat bekommen → [...], ob ihr Freund den Brief bekommen hat.

a. schön / das Wetter / am Wochenende / wird

→ Sie weiß nicht, ob ....

b. am Samstag / ihr Bruder / kann mitkommen

→ Sie weiß nicht, ob ....

c. deine Mutter / hat angerufen / er

→ Sie weiß nicht, ob ....

3 Invert the order of clauses. • •

a. Wir kommen pünktlich an, wenn es keinen Verkehr gibt.

→ ....

b. Bevor wir anfangen, möchte ich meine Mutter anrufen.

→ ....

c. Wir können dich nach Hause fahren, nachdem wir Sabine zum Bahnhof gebracht haben.

→ ....

Subordinating conjunctions

Conjunctions are words that link two clauses. Coordinating conjunctions (e.g. **und** *and*, **aber** *but*, **oder** *or*, **denn** *as, because*) link clauses of the same type and do not affect word order. Subordinating conjunctions, on the other hand, introduce a subordinate clause (separated from the main clause by a comma) and thus their use requires that the conjugated verb move to the last position in the subordinate clause. Here is a list of these (note that not all function as conjunctions in English).

als	*when*
anstatt	*instead of*
bevor	*before*
bis	*until*
da	*since*
damit	*so that*
dass	*that*
nachdem	*after, when*
ob	*whether, if*
obwohl	*although*
ohne dass	*without*
weil	*because*
wenn	*if, when, whenever*

- The conjunctions **da** and **weil** both express cause, but their use and meaning are not completely identical. (However, in spoken German, as in English, this difference in meaning is not always respected.)

  - **da** usually comes at the beginning of the sentence and introduces something that is relatively obvious or unsurprising, corresponding to *since* (in the sense of *because*): **Da es immer noch kalt ist, ziehe ich mich warm an.** *Since it is still cold, I am dressing warm.*

  - **weil** generally comes after the main clause in a sentence and introduces something that is unknown or less expected: **Ich ziehe mich warm an, weil es heute viel kälter ist.** *I am dressing warm because it is much colder today.*

- Another way to express cause is with the coordinating conjunction **denn** *as, for* (in the sense of *because*): **Ich ziehe mich warm an, denn es ist kalt.** *I'm dressing warm as it is cold.* However, as it is a coordinating conjunction the verb stays in second position – it doesn't affect the word order.

4 Circle the correct conjunction. ••

a. Er ist arbeiten gegangen, **obwohl / damit / bevor** er krank ist.

b. Putz dir die Zähne, **bevor / bis / damit** du ins Bett gehst!

c. Er sagt, **dass / damit / bis** es nicht wahr ist.

d. Ich helfe dir, **bevor / damit / obwohl** es schneller geht.

e. Ich werde lernen, **bevor / bis / dass** ich es sehr gut kann.

f. Ich würde öfter schwimmen gehen, **wenn / obwohl / ob** das Schwimmbad nicht so weit wäre.

g. Ich bin nicht sicher, **ob / wenn / damit** er meine Mail bekommen hat.

5 Complete the sentences with *da*, *weil* or *denn*.

a. Ich fahre mit dem Bus, ... ich einen Autounfall hatte.

b. .... wir wenig Zeit haben, werden wir nur die Familie besuchen.

c. Ich muss nach Hause, ... es ist schon spät.

d. Er kommt nicht, ... er krank ist.

Compound adjectives

As with nouns, adjectives in German can be turned into compound words by combining two terms or more. There are various possibilities, e.g.:

- adjective + adjective:
  dunkel *dark* + **rot** *red* →
  dunkelrot *dark red*

- noun + adjective:
  der Himmel *sky* + **blau** *blue* →
  himmelblau *sky blue*

In some cases, a letter is added (usually an **s**) or deleted (usually an **n**) between the words: **das Leben** *life* + **notwendig** *essential* → **lebensnotwendig** *vital, necessary for life*.

The noun in these compound words is not capitalized because it is used in an adjective.

6 Form compound adjectives from these words and then give their English equivalents.

a. der Schnee *snow* + **weiß** *white*

→ ....

b. hell *light* + **grün** *green*

→ ....

c. der Rabe *raven* + **schwarz** *black*

→ ....

d. das Haus *house* + **gemacht** *made*

→ ....

e. das Leben *life* + **froh** *glad*

→ ....

f. die See *sea* + **krank** *ill*

→ ....

7 Break these adjectives into their component words and then connect each to its equivalent in English.

1. strohdumm → .... •
2. kinderleicht → .... •
3. riesengroß → .... •
4. pflegeleicht → .... •
5. farbenblind → .... •
6. bildhübsch → .... •
7. federleicht → .... •

- **a**. pretty as a picture
- **b**. gigantic
- **c**. colour-blind
- **d**. child's play / really easy
- **e**. light as a feather
- **f**. low-maintenance
- **g**. thick as two short planks

Media and new technology

German has borrowed many new technology terms from English, but terms for older technology and media often differ between the two languages.

With loanwords, there is no definite rule for the grammatical gender – some terms may even have two genders – so you just have to learn these through practice.

8 Here are some typical phrases from a telephone conversation. Complete them using the words below.

Hallo zurückrufen **Telefonnummer** am Apparat
Nachricht verwählt **auf Wiederhören** **Vorwahl**

a. Guten Tag, Schmitt .... Könnte ich bitte mit Frau Köhler sprechen?

b. Einen Augenblick bitte. (...) Die Leitung ist besetzt. Könnten Sie später .... ?

c. Mit wem möchten Sie sprechen? (...) Sie haben sich .... Hier ist die 124.

d. Meine .... ist die 654 786 und die .... für Frankreich ist die 00 33.

e. Frau Köhler ist nicht da. Möchten Sie eine .... hinterlassen?

f. .... ! Wer ist bitte am Apparat?

g. In Ordnung. Morgen schicke ich Ihnen die ganze Information. .... !

9 Fill in the missing letters in the following words.

a. _ _ _ _ _ _ **H** _ **N** *television*

b. _ **A** _ _ _ *radio*

c. _ _ _ **H** *book*

d. _ _ _ **E** _ *letter* (message)

e. _ _ _ **T** _ _ **G** *newspaper*

f. **Z** _ _ _ **S** _ **H** _ _ **F** _ *magazine*

g. **N A** _ _ **R I** _ _ **T** _ _ *news*

h. **T** _ **G** _ **S** _ _ **H** _ **U** *news programme*

10 *Der, die* or *das?*

a. .... Handy

b. .... iPhone

c. .... Computer

d. .... / .... SMS

e. .... Website

f. .... / .... Mail

g. .... PC

h. .... Mailbox

i. .... Email Adresse

j. .... Keyboard

k. .... / .... Laptop

l. .... Informatik

m. .... Programm

n. .... Dokument

11 Connect each word to its translation.

1. die Verbindung •

2. der Drucker •

3. die Datei •

4. das Kennwort •

5. die Maus •

6. das Mauspad •

7. der Bildschirm •

• **a.** password

• **b.** mouse

• **c.** screen

• **d.** connection

• **e.** printer

• **f.** file

• **g.** mouse pad

Schön! You've completed Lesson 13. It's time to count up the icons for the exercises and record your results here and in the table on page 128.

14

Modal verbs

Modal verbs

These are auxiliary verbs that indicate ability, permission, obligation or attitude towards an action. They don't express the action itself, so are very often used with an infinitive, which goes to the end of the sentence. There are six modal verbs:

- **müssen** *to have to* ('must') expresses a strong obligation: **Wir müssen das Auto stehen lassen; es ist kaputt.** *We have to leave the car here; it has broken down.* **Der Film ist toll. Du musst ihn sehen**. *The film is great. You must see it.*

- **sollen** *to be supposed to* ('should', 'ought to') expresses a feeling of moral obligation to do something, either by someone else or by one's own conscience: **Du sollst dir die Zähne putzen**. *You should brush your teeth.* It can be softened by using the subjunctive II to convey a conditional sense: **Das sollte man nicht tun**. *One shouldn't do that.*

- **können** *to be able to* ('can') expresses capability or possibility: **Kannst du Deutsch (sprechen)?** *Can you speak German?* When requesting someone to do something or replying to a request, **können** is often in the subjunctive II to convey a conditional or a softer sense: **Könnten Sie früher kommen?** *Could you come earlier?* **Ja, ich könnte schon um 7 Uhr kommen**. *Yes, I could come as early as 7 o'clock.*

- **dürfen** *to be allowed to* ('may') expresses permission: **Ich darf bis Mitternacht ausgehen**. *I can stay out until midnight.* It is also a polite way to ask for something: **Darf ich Sie um das Salz bitten?** *May I ask you for the salt?* Although *can* and *may* are often used interchangeably in English, in German they are not. Thus 'mustn't' is **nicht dürfen**: **Du darfst das nicht machen**. *You mustn't do that.*

- **wollen** *to want, to want/wish to*: **Ich will es versuchen**. *I want to try it.*

- **mögen** *to like* is often used in the present tense in the context of food (without another verb): **Ich mag Schokoladenkuchen**. *I like chocolate cake.* In the subjunctive II, it expresses a wish, equivalent to the conditional *would like*: **Ich möchte zu Hause bleiben**. *I would like to stay at home.*

Note that the (non-modal) verb **wissen** *to know* conjugates like a modal verb (see the conjugation tables, pp. 118–119).

The usage between English and German is similar for most of the modal verbs, but remember not to confuse **können** and **dürfen**: **Er kann nicht mitkommen**. *He can't come.* (is unable to) whereas **Er darf nicht mitkommen**. *He may not come.* (is not allowed).

1 Circle the appropriate modal verb.

a. Vorm Essen **soll / kann / darf** man sich die Hände waschen.

b. Gestern **mochte / konnte / musste** ich um 4.30 aufstehen, weil ich einen frühen Flieger hatte.

c. **Will / Soll / Darf** ich Sie etwas fragen?

d. Wir **dürfen / sollen / können** hier nicht rauchen. Hier steht »Rauchen verboten!«

e. Er **will / darf / kann** sehr gut Deutsch.

f. **Müssen / Dürfen / Möchten** Sie etwas trinken? – Ja gern.

g. Ich **kann / muss / will** leider nicht länger bleiben. Mein Zug fährt in 30 Minuten.

h. **Kannst / Weißt / Darfst** du, wie spät es ist?

2 Circle the appropriate modal verb.

a. Er **darf/kann** nicht ins Kino gehen. *(It's against his parents' wishes.)*

b. ≠ Er **darf/kann** nicht ins Kino gehen. *(He has too much work to do.)*

c. Er **will/möchte** Wasser. *(He wants water and nothing else will do.)*

d. ≠ Er **will/möchte** Wasser. *(He would like water.)*

e. Er **soll/muss** es ihm sagen. *(It's impossible to hide the truth.)*

f. ≠ Er **soll/muss** es ihm sagen. *(It would be more proper.)*

3 Complete these sentences beginning with *Könnten Sie bitte...* [Could you please...] with one of the following verbs.

halten buchstabieren ausfüllen rufen wiederholen warten

a. Ich habe Sie nicht verstanden. Könnten Sie das bitte .... ?

b. Könnten Sie mir bitte ein Taxi .... ?

c. Könnten Sie bitte dieses Formular .... ?

d. Könnten Sie bitte Ihren Namen .... ?

e. Könnten Sie bitte einen Augenblick .... ?

f. Könnten Sie bitte die Klappe* .... ?

*Could you please shut up?

Expressions using modal verbs

In German there are quite a few idioms that contain a modal verb. Their primary meaning is therefore not always easy to discover, all the more so since often their English translation may use a different modal or not include one at all. Try and work out the following examples.

4 Connect each expression to its equivalent.

1. Es kann sein. •
2. Das darf doch nicht wahr sein. •
3. Wenn ich bitten darf. •
4. Was darf es sein? •
5. Wenn es sein muss! •
6. Wer will, der kann. •

• **a.** May I help you?
• **b.** If I may ...
• **c.** Maybe.
• **d.** Where there's a will there's a way!
• **e.** This is just unreal.
• **f.** If need be.

either ... or, neither ... nor, both ... and

- **entweder... oder** *either... or*: **Wir sehen uns entweder am Samstag oder am Sonntag.** *We'll see each other either on Saturday or on Sunday.*

- **weder... noch** *neither... nor*: **Sie kann weder Ski fahren noch Tennis spielen.** *She can neither ski nor play tennis.*

- **sowohl... als/wie auch** *both... and*: **Sowohl die Eltern als auch die Kinder dürften teilnehmen.** *Both the parents and the children can participate.*

5 Translate these sentences that contain modal verbs using the correlative conjunctions above.

a. She's allowed neither to go out **(ausgehen)** nor to invite friends.

→ ....

b. You must call him, either this evening or tomorrow at noon.

→ ....

c. She can speak both Italian and English.

→ ....

d. I would like either a chocolate ice cream or a chocolate cake.

→ ....

Trains and travel

Here are some useful terms and abbreviations if you're travelling by train in Germany: **Abf. →
Abfahrt** *Departure*, **Ank. → Ankunft** *Arrival*, **Hbf.
→ Hauptbahnhof** *central station*, **DB → Deutsche
Bahn** *German railway company*, **IC → InterCity**
and **EC → EuroCity** *regional network trains*, **ICE
→ InterCityExpress** *high-speed train*, **S-Bahn →
Schnellbahn** *rapid transit suburban train*.

6 Find a synonym for each of these words.

a. die Bahn

→ ....

b. der Flieger

→ ....

c. das Auto

→ ....

d. das Boot

→ ....

7 Match the words with their German terms: *crossroad/intersection, traffic light, traffic jam, traffic, accident, petrol/gas station.*

a. die Kreuzung → ....

b. der Unfall → ....

c. der Verkehr → ....

d. der Stau → ....

e. die Ampel → ....

f. die Tankstelle → ....

8 Fill in the missing letters.

a. die **H _ L T _ S _ E _ L _** *bus stop*

b. der **A _ _ _ _ _ _** *bus*

c. die **_ – B _ _ N** *underground train*

d. die **S _ _ _ _ _ _** *station*

e. das **_ _ _ O _ R _ D** *motorcycle*

f. die **S _ _ _ _ E _ B _ _ _** *tram*

g. die **_ _ T _ _ A _ _** *motorway/highway*

h. die **_ _ _ _ _ E** *road*

9 Fill in the crossword.

	1	2	3	4	5	6	7
A							
B							
C							
D							
E							
F							
G							
H							
I							
J							
K							

↓ **Down**

1A to fly

4D to run (a race)

6F to sail

→ **Across**

1B to run / to walk quickly

1E to go (on foot)

2I to land

1K to go by transport / to drive

Gut gemacht! You've completed Lesson 14. It's time to count up the icons for the exercises and record your results here and in the table on page 128.

15

Verbs with prefixes

Inseparable and separable prefixes

Many German verbs include prefixes that qualify the meaning. They are not so different from English prepositional verbs (e.g. *to pick up*, *to come in*, *to go out*, etc.), although in German the prefix is attached to the verb. Separable prefixes then detach when the verb is conjugated and go to the end of the clause.

- Inseparable prefixes never separate from the verb. They are: **be-, emp-, ent-, er-, ge-, miss-** (**miß-** pre-spelling reform), **ver-, voll-*** and **zer-**. The past participle does not take **ge-**: **Ich habe mein Fahrrad** verkauft. *I've sold my bicycle.* (**verkaufen**)

- Separable prefixes split from the verb in simple (one-word) tenses and go to the end of the clause. They are numerous: e.g. **an-, aus-, mit-, zurück-**, etc. When conjugated as a past participle, the **ge** is inserted between the prefix and the verb: an**kommen** → **Ich komme um 10 Uhr an.** → **Ich bin um 10 Uhr an**ge**kommen.**

- Dual prefixes can be either separable or inseparable depending on the context. These include **durch-, über-, unter-, um-, wider-** and **wieder-**. How do you know whether these prefixes separate or not? Many you'll have to pick up with practice, but here are a few tips. When **um-** expresses a change of place or state it is separable; when it has the sense of going 'around' something it is inseparable. When **wider-** is used in the sense of to 'reflect' or 'resound' it is separable; when it means 'against' it is inseparable. The prefix **wieder-** is almost always separable except in the verb **wiederholen** *to repeat*.

Note that the word stress falls on the prefix when it is separable, and on the base verb when it is inseparable.

* Since the last spelling reform, some verbal phrases treat **voll** as an adverb rather than a prefix. In this case it is separated from the verb (e.g. **voll füllen** *to fill up*).

I Conjugate these verbs to complete the sentences.

entdecken   **verbieten**   bekommen   **sich benehmen**
erzählen   **empfehlen**   **verstehen**   gewinnen

a. Ich habe nicht ...., was er gesagt hat.

b. Wer hat gestern beim Fußball ....

c. Rauchen .... Hast du das Schild nicht gesehen?

d. Was .... Sie mir als Wein?

e. Sie hat mir eine schöne Geschichte ....

f. Wie viele Mails .... du pro Tag?

g. In welchem Jahr wurde Amerika ....

h. Die Kinder haben sich sehr gut ....

2 Conjugate these verbs to complete the sentences.

anrufen   aussteigen   zurückkommen

einladen   vorbeigehen   aufräumen   mitbringen

50

a. Wen möchtest du zum Geburtstag ....?

b. Ich habe mein ganzes Zimmer ....

c. .... Sie bitte 2 Fotos und Ihren Pass ....?

d. Hast du etwas von Sabine gehört? – Ja, sie hat mich gestern ....

e. Wir .... bei der nächsten Bushaltestelle ....

f. Er ist an mir ...., ohne einmal zu grüßen.

g. Ich bin gestern aus dem Urlaub ....

3 Add (S) if the prefix is separable and (I) if it is inseparable.

a. unterschreiben *to sign* → ....
b. wiedersehen* *to see again* → ....
c. umziehen *to move house* → ....
d. überlegen *to think over* → ....
e. übersetzen *to translate* → ....
f. umfallen *to fall over* → ....

g. umarmen *to embrace* → ....
h. überholen *to overtake* → ....
i. unterbrechen *to interrupt* → ....
j. untergehen *to set/go down (sun)* → .....
k. umkehren *to turn around* → ....
l. durchqueren *to pass through* → ....

* This verb can also be written as two words: **wieder sehen**

4 Conjugate the appropriate verb to complete each sentence.

a. Es hat geklingelt. Kann jemand die Tür ....? **(machen / aufmachen / zumachen)**

b. Schnell, der Film hat schon .... **(fangen / anfangen / empfangen)**

c. Die Zeit .... schnell. **(gehen / vergehen / aufgehen)**

d. Viele alte Leute .... schlecht. **(hören / zuhören / gehören)**

e. Morgen möchte ich meine Großmutter .... **(suchen / versuchen / besuchen)**

f. Susi ist leider beim Abitur *(to fail the school-leaving exam)* .... **(fallen / umfallen / durchfallen)**

5 Derive the verbs from the nouns and vice versa.

Noun	Verb	Noun	Verb
die Abfahrt	....	....	erklären
die Ankunft	....	....	erzählen
die Bestellung	....	....	anfangen
die Unterschrift	....	....	wiederholen

6 Circle the correct word.

a. Es ist kalt. Zieh dir etwas Warmes **um / an / aus**!
It's cold. Put on something warm!

b. So kannst du nicht ausgehen. Zieh dich bitte **um / an / aus**!
You can't go out like that. Please change [your clothes]!

c. Zieh bitte die Schuhe **um / an / aus**!
Take off your shoes, please.

d. Ach! Ich habe 5 Kilo **zugenommen / aufgenommen / gewonnen**.
Oh! I've put on 5 kilos [11 pounds].

e. Du musst unbedingt **verlieren / abnehmen / wegnehmen**!
You absolutely must lose weight.

hin and *her*

These 'direction particles' indicate the direction of movement. They can be used as adverbs or separable prefixes with many verbs of movement, e.g. **gehen**, **kommen**, **fahren**, **bringen**, etc.

- **hin** generally indicates either movement away from the speaker (i.e. *there*) or destination: **Bring ihm den Wein hin!** *Take the wine over to him!* **Wo gehst du hin?/Wohin gehst du?** *Where are you going [to]?*

- **her** generally indicates either movement towards the speaker (i.e. *here*) or origin: **Bring mir den Wein her!** *Bring the wine over here!* **Wo kommt er her?/Woher kommt er?** *Where does he come from?*

hin and **her** can also be combined with adverbs or prepositions: **Ich bringe ihm den Wein hinauf.** *I'll take the wine up to him* ('there-up'). Colloquially, **hin** and **her** compound words are often contracted: **hinauf/herauf → rauf, hinaus/heraus → raus.**

Note this expression: **dieses ewige Hin und Her** *this continual to and fro ...*

7 Complete with *hin* or *her*. ●●

a. Komm ....! *Come here!*

b. Geh ....! *Go there!*

c. Geh .... ein!
   Ich bleibe draußen.
   Go in! I'm staying outside.

d. Ich bin oben.
   Komm .... auf!
   I'm upstairs. Come up!

e. Er kommt von dort ....
   He comes from there.

f. Bleib da.
   Ich fahre ....
   Stay there! I'll drive over.

Which 'but'?

The coordinating conjunction *but* is translated by either **aber** or **sondern**:

- **aber** links two clauses (positive or negative), providing contrasting additional information: **Ich war müde, aber ich konnte nicht schlafen.** *I was tired, but I couldn't sleep.* **Er ist nicht groß, aber er ist stark.** *He isn't big, but he's strong.*

- **sondern** introduces a rectification after a negative phrase, in the sense of *but rather*: **Das Konzert ist nicht am Sonntag, sondern am Samstag.** *The concert is not on Sunday but on Saturday.*

8 Complete with *aber* or *sondern*. ●●

a. Es war kurz, ... schön.

b. Es ist anstrengend, ... es macht mir Spaß.

c. Sie ist nicht 10, ... 11.

d. Ich komme nicht morgen, ... übermorgen.

e. Wir haben uns nicht lange gesehen, ... wir haben uns gut unterhalten.

f. Sie ist nicht Deutsche, ... Österreicherin.

Adverbs

One handy aspect of German is that in most cases, the same word can be used as an adjective or adverb: **gut** *good* or *well*; **schnell** *fast* or *quickly*. Plus, adverbs don't decline. Often adverbs are placed at the beginning of the clause; in this case the subject and verb must swap places so the verb is in second position: **Ich <u>komme</u> morgen, um dir zu helfen.** → Morgen <u>komme</u> ich, um dir zu helfen.

9 Connect each adverb of time to its translation.

1. jetzt •
2. bald •
3. schon •
4. später •
5. sofort •
6. noch •
7. früher •

• **a**. already
• **b**. earlier
• **c**. still
• **d**. now
• **e**. soon
• **f**. later
• **g**. immediately

10 Connect each adverb of manner to its translation.

1. wirklich •
2. kaum •
3. fast •
4. zusammen •
5. langsam •
6. ganz •
7. vorsichtig •

• **a**. carefully
• **b**. together
• **c**. completely
• **d**. slowly
• **e**. really
• **f**. almost
• **g**. barely/hardly

11 Connect each adverb of frequency to its translation.

1. immer •
2. oft •
3. gewöhnlich •
4. manchmal •
5. selten •
6. nie(mals) •
7. normalerweise •

• **a**. seldom/rarely
• **b**. never
• **c**. usually
• **d**. always
• **e**. often
• **f**. normally
• **g**. sometimes

Let's talk money

The next page has some useful vocabulary for talking about money – you'll notice that many of the related verbs have prefixes. **Der Euro** (100th of which is **der Cent**) was adopted in 2002. One thing to note when using these terms is that they stay singular when used with a number: **fünf Euro** *five euros*. The rule is that a masculine or neuter noun expressing a unit of measurement or quantity does not become plural.

12 Connect each sentence to its translation and underline any prefixes in the verbs.

1. Ich habe 100€ ausgegeben. •
2. Ich habe 100€ gespart. •
3. Ich habe 100€ bezahlt. •
4. Ich habe 100€ aufs Konto überwiesen. •
5. Ich habe 100€ verdient. •

• **a**. I have spent €100.
• **b**. I have transferred €100 to the account.
• **c**. I have earned €100.
• **d**. I have saved €100.
• **e**. I have paid €100.

13 Fill in the crossword.

→ **Across**
4A money
1C cheap, inexpensive
3F bill, invoice
3I expensive

↓ **Down**
2A rich
4A wallet
7H poor
9D bank

	1	2	3	4	5	6	7	8	9	10
A										
B										
C										
D										
E										
F										
G										
H										
I										
J										

14 Give the English equivalent of these German expressions or explain what they mean.

a. Zeit ist Geld.
→ ....
....

b. Besser ein Mann ohne Geld als Geld ohne Mann.
→ ....
....

c. Geld allein macht nicht glücklich.
→ ....
....

d. Er schwimmt im Geld.
→ ....
....

Bravo! You've completed Lesson 15. It's time to count up the icons for the exercises and record your results here and in the table on page 128.

16

Prepositional verbs

Accusative or dative?

Many German verbs are followed by a preposition. Depending on the preposition, either the accusative or the dative is required.

- Verbs constructed with accusative prepositions (e.g. **für**, **um**, etc.) take the accusative: **Es handelt sich um <u>den</u> Autounfall.** *It concerns the car accident.*
- Verbs constructed with dative prepositions (e.g. **mit**, **von**, **nach**, etc.) take the dative: **Wir beginnen** mit <u>der</u> **Nummer drei.** *We begin with the number three.*
- Verbs constructed with two-way prepositions (e.g. **an**, **auf**, **in**, **über**, **vor**, etc.) take either the accusative or dative depending on the verb or context: **Erinnerst du dich** an <u>ihn</u>? *Do you remember him?* (acc.) **Ich hänge** an <u>ihm</u>. *I'm attached to him.* (dat.) Sometimes either case can be used for the same verb – one example is auf <u>sein</u> (acc.) or <u>seinem</u> (dat.) **Recht bestehen** *to insist on his rights.*

Note that in German the prepositions might not be the ones you expect – the best idea is to learn prepositional verbs as a unit, with the appropriate case. Furthermore, some verbs can be used with different prepositions: **sich** über **etwas freuen** (+ acc.) means *to be delighted with something*, whereas **sich** auf **etwas freuen** (+ acc.) means *to look forward to something.*

In a response to a question or statement with a prepositional verb, generally the prepositional phrase is not repeated word for word. Instead it is replaced with:

- preposition + personal pronoun in the case of a living thing: **Ich habe mich sehr <u>über Paul</u> geärgert.** *I was very annoyed with Paul.* **Ich habe mich auch <u>über ihn</u> geärgert.** *I was also annoyed with him.*
- **da-** + preposition (or **dar-** if the preposition begins with a vowel) in the case of something inanimate: **Hast du <u>nach deiner Note</u> gefragt?** *Have you asked for your grade/mark?* **Ja, ich habe <u>danach</u> gefragt.** *Yes, I asked for it.*

1 Complete with the appropriate preposition.

a. Ich danke dir .... das Geschenk.

b. Es riecht .... Wein.

c. Ich bitte dich .... etwas Geduld.

d. Es hängt nur .... dir ab.

e. Ich gratuliere dir ....m Geburtstag.

f. Wir sprechen .... die Ferien.

g. Wir haben .... Politik diskutiert.

h. Ich interessiere mich sehr ...... Popmusik.

2 Tick the correct word.

a. Ich denke an ☐ **dich**. ☐ **dir**.

e. Ich habe lange auf ☐ **dich** gewartet. ☐ **dir**

b. Man kann sich nicht auf ☐ **dich** verlassen. ☐ **dir**

f. Sie hat sich in ☐ **eine** Fee verwandelt. ☐ **einer**

c. Ich kümmere mich um ☐ **den** Garten. ☐ **dem**

g. Er ist in ☐ **dich** verliebt. ☐ **dir**

d. Antworte auf ☐ **meine** Frage. ☐ **meiner**

h. Es ändert nichts an ☐ **die** Sache. ☐ **der**

3 Replace the prepositional phrase with either a personal pronoun or with *da(r)-* + preposition.

a. Hast du dich <u>nach den Uhrzeiten erkundigt</u>?

→ Nein, ich werde mich morgen .... erkundigen.

b. Für mich ist es kein Problem. Ich bin <u>an die Hitze</u> gewöhnt.

→ Ich aber bin überhaupt nicht .... gewöhnt.

c. Ich habe <u>an den Chef</u> persönlich geschrieben.

→ Gute Idee. Ich werde auch .... schreiben.

d. Kannst du dich <u>an Sabine</u> erinnern?

→ .... nicht, aber an ihren Bruder.

e. Möchte keiner von euch <u>an der Versammlung</u> teilnehmen?

→ Doch, ich möchte .... teilnehmen.

Questions with prepositional verbs

To ask a question with a prepositional verb, the preposition comes first:

• When asking about a person, the construction is preposition + **wen** for verbs followed by the accusative (An <u>wen</u> schreibst du? *To whom are you writing?* An <u>den</u> **Chef**. *To the boss.*) or **wem** for verbs followed by the dative (Mit <u>wem</u> arbeitest du? *With whom do you work?* Mit <u>meinem</u> **Kollegen**. *With my colleague.*)

• When asking about something inanimate, the construction is wo- + preposition (or **wor-** for prepositions beginning with a vowel): **Wovon** hast du geträumt? *About what were you dreaming?* Von **den Ferien**. *About the holidays.*

4 Complete these questions containing prepositional verbs.

a. .... ist er gestorben? – An Krebs.

b. .... kannst du dich erinnern? – An Sabine.

c. .... ist er verantwortlich? – Er ist für Südamerika verantwortlich.

d. .... ist er verliebt? – In Martha.

e. .... möchten Sie anfangen? – Mit der Übersetzung, wenn's geht.

In addition ...

Some adjective and noun phrases require a specific preposition; these follow the same rules as when used with verbs.

5 Complete the sentences with these words. The prepositions they are used with are in the text.

einverstanden **weit** fertig

freundlich zufrieden stolz

a. Das hat du gut gemacht. Ich bin sehr .... auf dich.

b. Ich möchte einen neuen Computer kaufen. Bist du damit ....?

c. Dein Lehrer ist mit dir sehr .... Er sagt, du arbeitest gut und schnell.

d. Bist du mit den Hausaufgaben ....? – Nein, mir fehlt noch eine Aufgabe.

e. Wohnst du .... von der Stadtmitte? – Nein, 5 Minuten zu Fuß.

f. Ich kann nichts sagen. Zu mir war er immer ....

6 Connect each noun phrase with its equivalent.

1. die Verwandtschaft mit •   • **a.** hatred for
2. die Lust auf (+ acc.) •   • **b.** impact on
3. der Einfluss auf (+ acc.) •   • **c.** love for
4. der Hass gegen •   • **d.** belief in
5. der Kampf gegen •   • **e.** desire for
6. der Glaube an (+ acc.) •   • **f.** the fight against
7. die Hoffnung auf (+ acc) •   • **g.** kinship with
8. die Liebe zu •   • **h.** hope for

'To learn' and 'to teach'

- **etwas lernen** *to learn something*: **Peter lernt schwimmen.** *Peter is learning to swim.* The phrase **auswendig lernen** is *to learn by heart, to memorize.*

- **jemandem etwas beibringen** *to teach someone something* (**bei** is a separable prefix): **Er hat ihm Deutsch beigebracht.** *He taught him German.* You might also hear the less common **jemanden etwas lehren**: **Er hat ihn Deutsch gelehrt.** *'He has to-him learned …'.*

- **hören, dass** or **erfahren, dass**: *to learn that, to hear that*: **Ich habe gehört/erfahren, dass er nach Deutschland umgezogen ist.** *I heard that he has moved to Germany.*

7 Translate these sentences. • •

a. I heard that Sabine got married. *('has married')*

➜ ....

b. I would like to learn German.

➜ ....

c. She is teaching him to play tennis. **(Tennis spielen)** *(2 possibilities)*

➜ ....

➜ ....

d. I learn better in the morning than in the afternoon.

➜ ....

e. She teaches German to foreigners.

➜ ....

Ich bin, du bist...

8 Connect each prepositional expression with its equivalent. • •

1. Auf keinen Fall •
2. In jedem Moment •
3. Zu Fuß •
4. Zu Befehl •
5. Auf gut Glück •
6. Auf die Minute genau •

• **a.** To the minute
• **b.** On foot
• **c.** At your command / Yes, sir!
• **d.** With any luck
• **e.** At any time
• **f.** In no case / On no account

Going on a trip?

9 Complete the sentences with these words: ··

Flughafen   Fahrkarte

Gepäck   Fenster   Gang   Flug   Bahnhof   Ermäßigung   Gleis

a. Ihr Flieger ist um 18 Uhr. Sie müssen spätestens um 17 Uhr am .... sein.

b. Sie haben viel ...., drei Koffer und eine Reisetasche.

c. Möchten Sie am .... oder am .... sitzen?

d. Der .... dauert 2 Stunden.

e. Sie müssen schnell zum ...., ihr Zug ist in 20 Minuten. Er fährt von .... 5 ab.

f. Als Student haben Sie eine ....

g. Sie möchten eine .... hin und zurück nach Köln.

10 Fill in the crossword. ··

→ **Across**
4D village
6G customs
1J capital
7M tourist

↓ **Down**
1H flag
4A country
6C border
7I town, city
9D foreign country (abroad)

	1	2	3	4	5	6	7	8	9	10	11	12	13
A													
B													
C						G							
D									A				
E													
F													
G								L					
H													
I													
J	H						T						
K													
L													
M													

11 Translate these German tourist locations.

a. der Schwarzwald → ....

b. der Bodensee → ....

c. der Kölner Dom → ....

d. der Bayerische Wald → ....

e. das Brandenburger Tor → ....

f. die Berliner Mauer → ....

g. die Ostsee → ....

h. die Nordsee → ....

12 Put the letters into the correct order to find the German words.

a. journey E / S / I / R / E

→ die ....

b. holidays N / F / R / I / E / E

→ die ....

c. vacation R / B / L / U / U / A

→ der ....

d. identity card W / S / A / I / U / E / S

→ der ....

e. passport E / I / S / P / S / A / S / R / E

→ der ....

f. surcharge G / U / Z / H / L / C / S / A

→ der ....

g. plane ticket T / C / K / F / G / I / L / E / T / U

→ das ....

h. stay, visit F / H / T / L / N / A / U / E / A / T

→ der ....

Well done! You've reached the end of Lesson 16. It's time to count up the icons for the exercises and record your result here and in the table on page 128.

17
Infinitives

Infinitives

When two verbs are used to express something, the dependent verb is an infinitive (i.e. unconjugated) and goes to the end of the sentence.

- Often, the infinitive is preceded by **zu** *to*: **Er versucht, früher zu kommen.** *He's trying to come earlier.* ('He tries earlier to come.')

  With separable-prefix verbs, **zu** is inserted between the prefix and the verb: **Er versucht, früher loszufahren.** *He's trying to leave earlier.*

- There are certain verbs after which the dependent infinitive is never preceded by **zu**. These include modal verbs as well as **bleiben, gehen, hören, lassen, lernen** and **sehen**: **Ich möchte ein Bier trinken.** *I'd like to drink a beer.* **Wir gehen später einkaufen.** *We're going shopping later.*

  With **helfen**, usually there is no **zu** unless there are at least two complements of the verb: **Ich helfe ihr abdecken.** *I'm helping her clear.* (1: *her*), but **Ich helfe ihr, den Tisch abzudecken.** *I'm helping her clear the table.* (2: *her* & *the table*).

  Note: **lassen** + infinitive is often used with the meaning *to have something done*: **Ich lasse mir die Haare schneiden.** *I'm having my hair cut.*

- A dependent infinitive can also be introduced by **um... zu** *in order to*, **ohne... zu** *without* and **anstatt... zu** *instead of*. In these cases, **zu** always comes directly before the infinitive, and if there is any other information it is placed between **um/ohne/anstatt** and **zu**: **Sie kam ins Haus, ohne zu klingeln.** *She came into the house without ringing [the bell].* **Sie ist früher gekommen, um die Kinder zu sehen.** *She came earlier in order to see the children.* These dependent clauses can also start the sentence, in which case the main clause must begin with the verb: **Ohne zu klingeln, <u>kam</u> er ins Haus.** (For more on word order, see Lesson 13.)

  Note: **um... zu** + infinitive can be used in response to questions asking **Wozu?** *For what? Why?*

I A *zu* or no *zu*? 😊

a. Ich lerne ...... schwimmen.

b. Er kann noch nicht richtig ...... laufen.

c. Ich freue mich, in Berlin ...... studieren.

d. Ich habe aufgehört ...... rauchen.

e. Ich hoffe, dich bald wieder ...... sehen.

f. Ich helfe dir, den Koffer ...... tragen.

g. Ich höre ihn ...... lachen.

2 Complete the sentences with *um... zu, anstatt... zu* or *ohne... zu.*

a. Lern für deine Prüfung, ... nichts .... machen.

b. Ich lebe nicht .... arbeiten, sondern ich arbeite .... leben.

c. .... mich .... fragen, hat er meine Tasche genommen.

d. Er ist gegangen, ... ein Wort .... sagen.

e. ...... richtig Deutsch .... lernen, solltest du ein Jahr in Deutschland verbringen.

f. Er macht seine Hausaufgaben, ... überlegen.

3 Match the answers to the corresponding questions.

1. Wozu brauchst du Seife? • • **a.** Um mir die Fingernägel anzumalen.
2. Wozu brauchst du Shampoo? • • **b.** Um mir die Haare zu föhnen.
3. Wozu brauchst du ein Handtuch? • • **c.** Um den Traumprinzen zu verführen. *(seduce)*
4. Wozu brauchst du Zahnpasta? • • **d.** Um mir die Haare zu waschen.
5. Wozu brauchst du einen Haartrockner? • • **e.** Um mich zu schminken.
6. Wozu brauchst du einen Lippenstift? • • **f.** Um mich zu waschen.
7. Wozu brauchst du einen Nagellack? • • **g.** Um mich abzutrocknen.
8. Wozu machst du dich so hübsch? • • **h.** Um mir die Zähne zu putzen.

Infinitives used as nouns

A German infinitive can be turned into a noun simply by capitalizing it. These nouns are neuter and typically translate to English gerunds (verbal nouns ending in *-ing*). They can express:

- a collective idea: **das Schreien der Kinder** *the shouting of children*

- the act of doing something: **Ich habe mir beim Essen in die Zunge gebissen.** *I bit my tongue while eating.* **Das Rauchen ist verboten.** *Smoking is prohibited.*

- the equivalent of an **um... zu** + infinitive clause: **Um zu übersetzen brauche ich ein Wörterbuch.** *In order to translate, I need a dictionary.* → **Zum Übersetzen brauche ich ein Wörterbuch.** *For translating, I need a dictionary.*

  Note: **zum** + verbal noun can be used in response to questions asking **Wozu?** *For what? Why?*: **Wozu brauchst du das Wörterbuch? – Zum Übersetzen.**

- the equivalent of a clause introduced by a conjunction: **Nachdem man aufgewacht ist, sollte man...** *After one wakes up one should ...* → **Nach dem Aufwachen sollte man...** *After waking one should ...*

Verbs used as nouns are often used in newspaper headlines and advertisements: **Deutsch lernen beim Schlafen** *Learn German while sleeping.*

4 Complete the newspaper headlines with one of the verbal nouns below.

Einkaufen

Abnehmen

Fahren

Warten

Essen

a
STUNDENLANGES
....
FÜR FUSSBALLKARTEN

Über 5 Stunden
mussten die Fans von...

b
WUNDERMEDIKAMENT
ZUM ....

Sie wog 80 kg und wiegt
heute nur noch...

c
WENIG ....
MACHT NOCH KEIN
SUPERMODEL

Wer ein Supermodel
sein möchte...

d
DAS .... IST
DAS LIEBSTE HOBBY
DER STARS

Sie haben Geld und gehen
in die schönsten Geschäfte.

e
BEIM ....
EINGESCHLAFEN

Auf der Autobahn
ist gestern...

5 Replace the subordinate clause with an infinitive used as a noun.

a. Ich brauche ein Glas, um zu trinken.

→ ....

b. Das ist eine schöne Wiese, um zu spielen.

→ ....

c. Bevor ich laufe, mache ich ein paar Sportübungen.

→ ....

d. Ich komme, nachdem ich trainiert habe.

→ ....

e. Er braucht einen Stock, um zu gehen.

→ ....

6 Match each question to its response.

1. Wozu brauchst du einen Pinsel? •
2. Wozu brauchst du einen Besen? •
3. Wozu brauchst du einen Kuli? •
4. Wozu brauchst du ein Lineal? •
5. Wozu brauchst du ein Rezeptbuch? •
6. Wozu brauchst du Mehl? •
7. Wozu brauchst du eine Schere? •
8. Wozu brauchst du eine Brille? •

• **a**. Zum Kochen.
• **b**. Zum Lesen.
• **c**. Zum Unterstreichen.
• **d**. Zum Schneiden.
• **e**. Zum Fegen.
• **f**. Zum Unterschreiben.
• **g**. Zum Backen.
• **h**. Zum Malen.

7 Give the infinitive of these simple past verbs.

a. fiel → ....
d. hob → ....
g. zog → ....

b. schlug → ....
e. sprang → ....
h. schnitt → ....

c. brach → ....
f. verlor → ....
i. stieg → ....

Comma usage

The rules for when commas are required in German sentences have been relaxed by the latest spelling reforms, but there are contexts in which they are obligatory. A dependent clause is always preceded by a comma. However, with infinitive clauses the rule varies:

• Typically, there is no comma before **zu** + infinitive if the infinitive has no complement: **Er versucht zu kommen.** *He is trying to come.*

  But if any confusion is possible, a comma is used: **Er versucht, nicht zu laufen.** *He's trying not to run.* **Er versucht nicht, zu laufen.** *He's not trying to run.*

• If **zu** + infinitive has at least one complement, a comma precedes the clause: **Er versucht, einen früheren Zug zu nehmen.** *He's trying to catch an earlier train.*

• With **um... zu, ohne... zu, anstatt... zu** + infinitive, a comma is always required to separate the clauses: **Sie ist zu Hause geblieben, anstatt mit ihrer Familie in Urlaub zu fahren.** *She stayed at home instead of going on vacation with her family.* **Ohne zu klingeln, kam sie ins Haus.** *Without ringing the bell, she came into the house.*

8 Add a comma if necessary.

a. Wir sind nach Berlin gefahren um meine Tante zu besuchen.

b. Wir planen nach Indien zu reisen.

c. Ich werde früher aus dem Büro gehen um ihn abzuholen.

d. Ich freue mich mit der ganzen Familie eine Woche in Wien zu verbringen.

e. Er betrat den Raum ohne mich zu grüßen.

f. Anstatt ein Geschenk zu kaufen werde ich ihm Geld geben.

g. Es beginnt zu regnen.

Saying 'to stop'

There are various verbs for *to stop* in German:

- **aufhören** is the most common, used for:
  - stopping any action in general (e.g. work, a game, a dispute, a behaviour, etc.): **Er hört nicht auf zu arbeiten.** *He doesn't stop working.* **Hör auf, deinen Bruder zu ärgern.** *Stop annoying your brother.* **Hör auf!** *Stop it!*
  - cessation of an event in the broad sense of the term, e.g. a weather phenomenon, noise, etc.: **Es regnet, ohne aufzuhören.** *It's raining non-stop* ('without stopping'). **Das Geräusch hörte plötzlich auf.** *The noise suddenly stopped.*
- **anhalten** is used for:
  - deliberately stopping [in] a vehicle: **Ich kann nicht mitten auf der Autobahn anhalten.** *I can't stop in the middle of the motorway.*
- **stoppen** is used in the sense of bringing something to a standstill (and is sometimes synonymous with **anhalten**): **Wir müssen diese Entwicklung stoppen.** *We must stop this development.* **Das Auto hat vor der Kreuzung gestoppt.** *The car stopped at the intersection.* **den Ball stoppen** *to stop the ball.*
- **stehen bleiben*** is used:
  - when a pedestrian stops: **Er blieb vor jedem Schaufenster stehen.** *He stopped in front of each shop window.*
  - when something stops working; a breakdown in a mechanism such as a watch or a vehicle: **Meine Uhr ist stehen geblieben.** *My watch has stopped.*
  - when a discussion or a lecture has been interrupted: **Wo sind wir letztes Mal stehen geblieben?** *Where did we leave off last time?*

*Conjugation: **ich bleibe stehen** / *stop*, **ich blieb stehen** / *stopped*, **ich bin stehen geblieben** / *have stopped*, etc.

9 Complete the sentences by adding the appropriate verb.

a. .... zu weinen.

b. Wir müssen an der nächsten Tankstelle ....

c. Als der Busfahrer das Kind sah, ... er ....

d. Der Motor machte ein komisches Geräusch und plötzlich ....
das Auto ....

e. Seit drei Tagen .... es nicht .... zu schneien.

10 Translate these sentences.

a. I stop playing. → ....

....

b. Stop! *(informal sing.)* I can't walk so
fast. → ....

....

c. Stop! *(informal sing.)* It's red. → ....

....

d. Stop *(informal sing.)* eating chocolate.

→ ....

....

e. The referee **(der Schiedsrichter)** stopped
the game. → ....

....

....

11 Match each expression to its equivalent.

1. zum Glück ●

2. zum Wohl ●

3. zum Teil ●

4. zum verrückt werden ●

5. zum Schreien ●

6. zum letzten Mal ●

● **a.** partly

● **b.** Cheers!

● **c.** for the last time

● **d.** [it's] a scream/hilarious

● **e.** luckily

● **f.** [enough] to drive you crazy

Großartig! You've reached the end
of Lesson 17. It's time to count
up the icons for the exercises and
record your result here and in the
table on page 128.

18

Showing possession

Possessive adjectives and pronouns

These indicate who something belongs to. In German, they need to agree with the gender, number and case of the 'possessed' object.

- Possessive adjectives are used before a noun. In the nominative masculine, they are: **mein** *my*, **dein** *your*, **sein** *his/its*, **ihr** *her/its, their*, **unser** *our*, **euer** *your* (pl.), **Ihr** *your* (formal). They decline following the pattern of **ein/kein** (see declension type III, p. 120): **mein Vater** *my father* (m.), **meine Mutter** *my mother* (f.), **mein Kind** *my child* (n.), **meine Eltern** *my parents* (pl.) (nominative).

  Note that the third-person singular **sein** refers to a possessor that is either masculine (e.g. **Herr Müller** or **der Baum** *tree*) or neuter (e.g. **das Kind** *child* or **das Dorf** *village*). The third-person **ihr** refers to a feminine possessor (e.g. **Frau Ulm** or **die Erde** *the Earth*) or more than one possessor (*their*). It's capitalized for the formal *your*.

- Possessive pronouns are used on their own to replace a noun: **meiner** *mine*, **deiner** *yours*, **seiner** *his*, **ihrer** *hers, theirs*, etc. (if the object possessed is masculine singular and the subject of the sentence) (see table, p. 121). They are formed from the masculine nominative possessive adjectives plus the case endings for the definite article **der**, **die** or **das** (see declension type I, p. 120): **Meiner ist alt. Meine ist alt. Mein(e)s ist alt. Meine sind alt.** *Mine is/are old.* (nominative, referring to something that is masculine, feminine, neuter, plural).

Lastly, don't forget the genitive or **von** + dative for showing possession (see Lesson 11).

---

1 Complete with the possessive adjectives in the nominative.

a. ich → .... Bruder

b. ihr → .... Kinder

c. sie → .... Vater

d. du → .... Schwester

e. er → .... Tochter

f. wir → .... Kind

2 Complete with the appropriate possessive adjectives.

a. Der Junge spielt mit .... Freunden.

b. Ich besuche .... Freundin.

c. Sabine und .... Kinder kommen morgen an.

d. Hast du .... Klavierlehrerin angerufen?

e. Wie lange wart ihr bei .... Großeltern?

f. Wir können .... Tochter zum Bahnhof bringen.

3 Translate these sentences depending on who the friend is.

a. Sabine is at her boyfriend's. → ....

b. Paul is also at her boyfriend's. *(Sabine's boyfriend)* → ....

c. Paul calls his friend *(m.)*. → ....

d. Paul calls his girlfriend. → ....

e. Sabine calls her friend *(f.)*. → ....

f. Sabine calls his friend *(m.)*. *(Paul's friend)* → ....

g. Sabine calls his girlfriend. *(Paul's girlfriend)* → ....

h. Paul is also at her friend's *(f.)*. *(Sabine's friend)* → ....

4 Change the sentences following the example.
E.g. Das ist <u>mein Bruder</u>. → Das ist <u>meiner</u>.

a. Das ist seine Schwester. → Das ist ....

b. Das ist unser Sohn. → Das ist ....

c. Das sind eure Eltern. → Das sind ....

d. Das ist dein Kind. → Das ist ....

e. Das ist meine Frau. → Das ist ....

f. Das sind eure Eltern. → Das sind ....

5 Complete the sentences with a possessive pronoun.
E.g. Ich übernachte bei <u>meiner Tante</u>, und du bei <u>deiner</u>.

a. Er arbeitet mit seinem Lehrer, und sie mit ....

b. Ich mache es für meinen Sohn, und du für ....

c. Wir rufen unsere Eltern an, und ihr ....

d. Ich schreibe meiner Mutter, und Sie ....

e. Du bleibst bei deinem Bruder, und er bei ....

Saying 'only'

In German, *only* is expressed with either **erst** or **nur** depending on the context.

- **erst** is used to convey a temporary constraint that will change in time. It implies that there is more to come:
  Er ist erst fünf Jahre alt. *He's only five years old.*
  Ich habe erst zehn Seiten gelesen. *I have read only ten pages.*
  Es ist erst 10 Uhr. *It's only 10:00.*

  erst is often used subjectively – its opposite is **schon**.
  Ich habe erst zwei Maß getrunken! *I've only drunk two litres of beer!*
  Hast du schon zwei Maß getrunken? *You've already drunk two litres of beer?*

- **nur** is used to convey a definitive constraint that is not expected to change. One of its uses is in the sense of 'not more than':
  Ich kann nur einen Tag bleiben. *I can stay only one day.*
  Ich habe nur ein kleines Haus. *I have only a small house.*
  Sie will nur schlafen. *She only wants to sleep.*

- Sometimes **erst** conveys an expectation on the speaker's part referring to time, expressing the idea of *no sooner than, not until, only when*:
  Er kommt erst am Sonntag. *He's only arriving on Sunday.*
  Erst wenn du kommst, essen wir. *We won't eat until you arrive.*

6 *Erst* or *nur*? ●●

a. Wir haben Zeit. Es ist .... 7 Uhr.

b. Ich brauche .... 5 Minuten bis zur Schule.

c. Bist du mit dem Buch fertig? – Nein, ich habe .... ein Kapitel gelesen.

d. Leider habe ich .... eine Woche Urlaub.

e. Sie war .... 17, als sie ihn heiratete.

f. Ich habe .... 5 Euro bei mir.

7 Explain the difference in meaning between the following sentences. ●●

a. Wir sind erst 100 km gefahren. / Wir sind nur 100 km gefahren.
→ .... / ....

b. Er hat erst eine Seite geschrieben. / Er hat nur eine Seite geschrieben.
→ .... / ....

c. Er kommt erst morgen. / Er kommt nur morgen.
→ .... / ....

'Beginning', 'middle' and 'end'

The corresponding nouns in German are **der Anfang** *beginning*, **die Mitte** *middle* and **das Ende** *end*. Here are some tips on their usage:

- They can be used on their own (without a preposition or article) with dates, the names of months or to indicate an approximate age: **Wir sind Ende 2011 umgezogen.** *We moved at the end of 2011.* **Ich komme Mitte Juni.** *I'm coming in mid-June.* **Er ist Anfang fünfzig.** *He's in his early 50s.*

- They are preceded by **am** or **in der** when used in a complement in the genitive: **am Anfang / in der Mitte / am Ende des Films** *at the beginning / in the middle / at the end of the film*. When combined with a time phrase, they can also stand alone: **Dies geschah (am) Anfang des Jahres.** *This happened at the beginning of the year.*

- Without a complement (i.e. not followed by a prepositional phrase, **Anfang** and **Ende** are preceded by **am**: **Am Anfang war alles in Ordnung.** *At the beginning everything was fine.*

- They can also be used with other prepositions (e.g. **gegen** *towards*, **seit** *since*, etc.): **Seit Anfang des Sommers ist er arbeitslos.** *Since the beginning of the summer he has been unemployed.* **Es war gegen Ende der neunziger Jahre.** *It was towards the end of the 90s.*

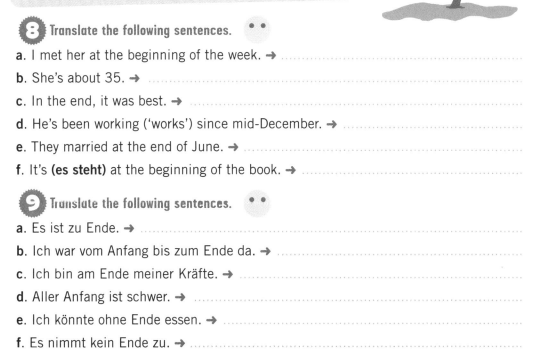

8 Translate the following sentences.

a. I met her at the beginning of the week. ➔ ....

b. She's about 35. ➔ ....

c. In the end, it was best. ➔ ....

d. He's been working ('works') since mid-December. ➔ ....

e. They married at the end of June. ➔ ....

f. It's **(es steht)** at the beginning of the book. ➔ ....

9 Translate the following sentences.

a. Es ist zu Ende. ➔ ....

b. Ich war vom Anfang bis zum Ende da. ➔ ....

c. Ich bin am Ende meiner Kräfte. ➔ ....

d. Aller Anfang ist schwer. ➔ ....

e. Ich könnte ohne Ende essen. ➔ ....

f. Es nimmt kein Ende zu. ➔ ....

Talking about one's family

Here are some terms for people in the extended family.

The term **die Schwiegerfamilie** equates to *in-laws*. The prefix **Schwieger-** is used to form most of the individual in-laws, e.g. **der Schwiegersohn** *son-in-law*; **die Schwiegertochter** *daughter-in-law*, etc. The exceptions: **der Schwager** *brother-in-law* and **die Schwägerin** *sister-in-law*

The grandchildren are **die Enkelkinder**, and so **der Enkel(-)** is *grandson(s)* and **die Enkelin(nen)** *granddaughter(s)*. **Der Neffe(n)** is *nephew(s)* and **die Nichte(n)** *niece(s)*. The prefix **Ur-** is equivalent to *great-*: **die Urgroßeltern** *great-grandparents*; **die Urenkel** *great-grandchildren*.

Complete the sentences with these family members:

die Schwiegereltern   die Cousine

die Schwägerin   der Onkel

der Enkel   der Schwiegervater

die Tante   der Schwager

die Enkelin   die Enkelkinder

die Schwiegermutter   der Cousin

der Neffe (x2)   die Nichte

die Großeltern   der Urgroßvater

a. Die Tochter meiner Schwester ist meine .... und ihr Sohn ist mein .... Der Sohn meines Bruders ist auch mein ....

b. Die Mutter meines Mannes ist meine .... und der Vater ist mein .... Beide sind meine ....

c. Mein Mann hat eine Schwester. Das ist meine .... Er hat auch einen Bruder. Das ist mein ....

d. Der Bruder meiner Mutter ist mein .... und die Schwester meiner Mutter ist meine ....

e. Der Bruder meiner Mutter hat eine Tochter und einen Sohn. Das sind meine .... und mein ....

f. Die Eltern meiner Mutter und meines Vater sind meine ....

g. Der Vater des Vaters meines Vaters ist mein ....

h. Meine Tochter ist die .... meiner Mutter und mein Sohn ist ihr ....

i. Meine Tochter hat 3 Kinder und mein Sohn 2, also habe ich 5 ....

Marriage

»Verliebt, verlobt, verheiratet« '*In love, engaged, married*' is a German expression. Perhaps it would be more topical to add **geschieden** *divorced* ... But before moving on to marriage statistics, do you know the terms **das Brautpaar**, **der Bräutigam**, **die Braut**, **das Brautkleid** and **der Ehering**? Test yourself by completing the following exercise!

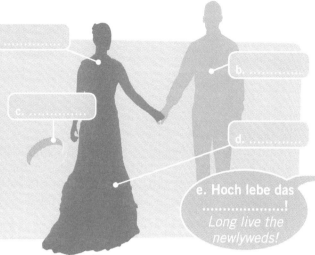

a. ....
b. ....
c. ....
d. ....

e. Hoch lebe das ....!
Long live the newlyweds!

 Use the terms below to complete the sentences.

a. 53% der Deutschen sind verheiratet. Männer .... im Schnitt *(on average)* mit 33,2 Jahren und Frauen mit 30,3 Jahren.

b. 27,7% der Frauen wünschen sich, dass der Mann einen .... macht.

c. In den letzten 50 Jahren hat sich die .... stark erhöht *(sharply increased)*. In den fünfziger Jahren gab es im Schnitt 8 .... für 1 Scheidung, heute lassen sich 40 bis 50% der Ehepaare scheiden. Meistens lassen sie sich nach 10 bis 15 Jahren..................... scheiden.

die Liebe auf den ersten Blick
love at first sight

Hochzeiten
weddings

heiraten
to marry

ihr erstes Kind bekommen
to have their first child

die Scheidungsrate
the divorce rate

der Heiratsantrag
marriage proposal

die Ehe
marriage, married life

d. In 53% der Familien lebt nur ein minderjähriges *(minor)* Kind, und die Frauen .... zwischen 28 und 29 Jahren. (im Schnitt)

e. Und nun eine wichtige Frage. Sind die Deutschen romantisch? Ja, denn 55% glauben an .... und 72% an die Liebe fürs Leben. Und Sie?

Well done! You've reached the end of Lesson 18. It's time to count up the icons for the exercises and record your result here and in the table on page 128.

19

Relative pronouns

Relative pronouns

A relative pronoun is used to introduce a clause that provides additional information about a noun or pronoun that has already been mentioned (e.g. *that, which, who,* etc.). In German, the forms are the same as the definite article (**der, die, das**), except for the dative plural and all genitive forms (see table, p. 121). The clause introduced by a relative pronoun is separated from the main clause by a comma.

The relative pronoun must agree in gender and number with the noun to which it refers, and its case depends on its grammatical function in the relative clause (whether it is a subject, direct or indirect object, the object of a preposition, etc.).

- If the relative clause doesn't start with a preposition:
  Der Junge, der bei uns wohnt, kommt aus Rom. *The boy who lives with us comes from Rome.* → der because (a) it refers to **der Junge** (masc. sing.), and (b) it is the subject of the relative clause (nominative)
  Die Frau, der du das Buch geschenkt hast, hat angerufen. *The woman to whom you gave the book phoned.* → der because (a) it refers to **die Frau** (fem. sing.), and (b) it is the indirect object of the relative clause (dative)

- If the relative clause starts with a preposition:
  Der Junge, mit dem du im Kino warst, ist mein Freund. *The boy who you were with in the cinema is my friend.* → dem because (a) it refers to **der Junge** (masc. sing.), and (b) it follows the preposition **mit** (dative)

Note: If the noun referred to is a geographical place, the relative pronoun needs to be one of the *where* adverbs (which don't decline): **wo** (location), **wohin** (destination) or **woher** (origin). Either a relative pronoun or a *where* adverb can be used to refer to a place in general: **Das ist das Restaurant, in dem/wo wir gestern waren.** *This is the restaurant where we were yesterday.*

I Complete these sentences with relative clauses.

a. Der Anzug, ... du gestern getragen hast, ist sehr schön.

b. Er möchte nach München, ... auch seine Geschwister studieren.

c. Kennst du den Jungen, in .... Sabine verliebt ist?

d. Die Leute, mit .... ich gesprochen habe, waren sehr freundlich.

e. Wer ist das Mädchen, ... gestern bei dir war?

2 Rewrite these sentences with relative clauses introduced by **wo, wohin** or **woher**.

a. Das Bett, in dem ich schlafe, ist nicht breit.

→ ....

b. Die Stadt, aus der ich komme, liegt im Norden.

→ ....

c. Das Restaurant, in das ich gehen wollte, hat zu.

→ ....

d. Das ist ein kleines Kino, in dem gute Filme laufen.

→ ....

The relative pronoun in the genitive

As the genitive indicates possession, this relative pronoun equates to *whose*. In German, it has two forms: **dessen** (if the possessor is a masculine or neuter singular noun) and **deren** (if it is a feminine or plural noun). These come before the 'possessed' noun, with no article. **Dieser Junge,** dessen **Mutter Sportlehrerin ist, hat das Rennen gewonnen.** *This boy, whose mother is a PE teacher, won the race.*

3 Add the appropriate relative pronoun in these genitive relative clauses.

a. Sabine, ... Bruder du getroffen hast, spielt im Orchester.

b. Der Schriftsteller, ... Novelle mir sehr gefallen hat, kommt heute in unsere Schule.

c. Die Kinder, ... Eltern kein Auto haben, können mit dem Bus fahren.

d. Peter, ... Vater als Übersetzer arbeitet, kann acht Sprachen.

4 Translate these sentences.

a. Peter is a student with whom I am very pleased. **(zufrieden mit)**

→ ....

b. Do you (**du**) know an actor whose name begins with D? **(der Schauspieler)**

→ ....

c. That's the film that won an Oscar. **(der Oscar)**

→ ....

d. He lives in Heidelberg, where I worked for 5 years. **(5 Jahre lang)**

→ ....

The indefinite relative pronouns *wer* and *was*

- The pronoun **wer** *whoever, anyone* refers to an undefined person, and **was** *that, what, whatever* to an unspecified thing. (For their forms, see p. 121.) As they are used to refer to an undefined noun, they cannot be replaced by **der**, **die** or **das**.
  Wer zu viel Alkohol trinkt, wird nicht mit dem Auto zurückfahren können.
  Anyone who drinks too much alcohol will not be able to drive back.
  Ich habe nicht gesehen, was sie gekauft hat. *I didn't see what she bought.*

- **was** is always used after the indefinite pronouns **alles** *all*, **nichts** *nothing*, **vieles** *much, a lot of*, **etwas** *something* and after the demonstrative **das**:
  Das ist alles, was ich habe. *That is all that* I have.*
  Das ist nicht genau das, was ich brauche. *That's not exactly what I need.*

- **was** is also required after a superlative when it is the last word in the main clause:
  Das ist das Schönste, was ich gesehen habe.
  That is the most beautiful thing that I have seen.

  But if a noun comes after the superlative, then a definite relative pronoun is used:
  Das ist das schönste Bild, das ich gesehen habe.
  That is the most beautiful picture that I have seen.

  * In English, relative pronouns are often omitted, but in German they are not.

5 Complete with *wer*, *was* or a definite relative pronoun.

a. .... er da gemacht hat, gefällt mir nicht.

b. .... gehen will, kann gehen.

c. Das ist etwas, ... ich nicht verstehe.

d. Das, ... du siehst, ist der Eiffelturm.

e. Das ist das billigste Hotel, ... ich gefunden habe.

f. .... nicht wagt *(dares)*, der gewinnt nicht.

g. Hast du alles, ... du brauchst?

Using *der*, *die*, *das* as a demonstrative

Although *this, these, that, those* in German are **dieser** (m.), **diese** (f. & pl.), **dieses** (n.), in speech the definite article (**der**, **die**, **das**) is often used. It declines like the relative pronoun (p. 121) and agrees with the noun to which it refers. Its usage differs somewhat from English – it basically accentuates the noun it refers to: **Uta hat einen Rotwein gekauft; der schmeckt gut.** *Uta bought a red wine; it's ('this is') good.*

6 Complete with a demonstrative pronoun (*der, die* or *das*). ••

a. Heute kommt meine Freundin Susi. – .... kenne ich doch.

b. Unsere deutschen Freunde sind zu Besuch; .... haben wir heute Versailles gezeigt.

c. Soll ich Peter zum Essen einladen? – Bitte nicht! .... mag ich überhaupt nicht.

d. Ich habe seinen letzten Roman gelesen; .... empfehle ich dir.

e. Unser Nachbar ist zum Glück ausgezogen. .... war so unfreundlich.

Saying 'to happen' and 'to manage to'

Let's look at some useful vocabulary that frequently crops up in conversations.

- **geschehen** *to happen, to occur, to take place* (**das Geschehen** *events*): **Der Unfall ist vor meinen Augen geschehen.** *The accident happened right before my eyes.*

- **passieren** *to happen* is a synonym: **Ihm ist etwas Schlimmes passiert.** *Something bad has happened to him.*

  Both these verbs form the present perfect with **sein**, and when they are used with an indirect object (*to happen to*), they take the dative (and sometimes **mit**): **Was ist (mit) ihm passiert/geschehen?** *What happened to him?* You might also hear **geschehen/passieren lassen** *to let something happen.*

- **Es kommt vor (, dass...)** (from the separable-prefix verb **vorkommen** *to happen*) means *It happens (that) ...* in the sense of 'it can happen' as well as 'sometimes', 'it's possible': **Es kommt vor, dass es sehr viel Stau gibt.** *Sometimes there's a lot of traffic.* **Das kommt nie wieder vor.** *It will never happen again.*

- **schaffen** means *to manage to* (among other things). It is always used with a direct object (in the accusative): **Heute schaffe ich es nicht, alles zu machen.** *Today I won't manage to do everything.* **Hast du es geschafft?** *Have you managed to do it?*

  (Careful! When **schaffen** means *to manage to*, it conjugates as **ich schaffte** (simple past), **geschafft** (past participle), whereas **schaffen** *to create* conjugates as **ich schuf, geschaffen**: **Und Gott schuf die Welt.** *And God created the world.*)

7 Complete with one of the verbs above. ••

a. Ich habe leider eine schlechte Note. – Das ist nicht schlimm. Es ....

b. Das ist .... , als ich aus dem Geschäft kam.

c. Ihm ist sicher ein Unglück *(misfortune)* ....

d. Ich werde es nie .... Das ist zu schwierig für mich.

e. Es .... dass es dabei Probleme gibt.

8 Translate these sentences.

a. Sometimes it snows in May. ➜ ....

b. What happened to you *(informal sing.)*? ➜ ....

c. When did that happen? ➜ ....

d. Great, you *(informal sing.)* managed it! ➜ ....

e. He never lets that happen. ➜ ....

The weather, the months & the seasons

Let's review some more useful vocabulary for conversations: **Wie ist das Wetter?** *How is the weather?* **Habt ihr schönes Wetter?** *Are you* (informal pl.) *having good weather?* **Der Wetterbericht** is *weather report*, **die Wettervorhersage** is *weather forecast* and **bei schechtem/schönem Wetter** means *in bad/good weather*. If you are particularly interested in knowing about the weather in the month of January in Austria, be aware that Austrians say **Jänner**, while Germans use a slightly different word that we will see in the following exercises.

9 List the number of each sentence under the picture it goes with. Some apply to more than one picture.

1. Die Sonne scheint.
2. Es ist kalt.
3. Es ist warm.
4. Es ist nebelig.
5. Es schneit.

6. Es ist windig.
7. Es regnet.
8. Es ist bewölkt
9. Es ist vereist.
10. Es ist heiß.

11. Es gibt ein Gewitter.
12. Er macht ein Gesicht wie drei Tage Regenwetter.
13. Bei diesem Wetter jagt man keinen Hund vor die Tür. *(It's not fit to send a dog out.)*

a. ....

b. ....

c. ....

d. ....

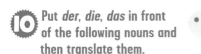 Put *der*, *die*, *das* in front of the following nouns and then translate them.

a. ...... Hitze → ....

b. ...... Klima → ....

c. ...... Regen → ....

d. ...... Temperatur → ....

e. ...... Schnee → ....

f. ...... Glatteis → ....

g. ...... Hagel → ....

h. ...... Wind → ....

i. ...... Blitz → ....

j. ...... Wetter → ....

k. ...... Regenbogen → ....

l. ...... Donner → ....

Fill in the crossword.

↓ Down
3J moon
5F sun
6J air
8D earth
10A planet

→ Across
6D star
4G cloud
1J sky

	1	2	3	4	5	6	7	8	9	10
A										
B										
C										A
D								E		
E										
F										
G			W							
H										
I				N						
J	H									
K						U				
L										
M			D							

Fill in the letters of the months and the seasons.

a. _ A _ U A _

b. _ E _ _ U A _

c. _ Ä _ _

d. A _ _ I _

e. _ A I

f. _ U _ I

g. _ U _ I

h. A U _ U _ _

i. _ E _ _ E _ _ E _

j. O _ _ O _ E _

k. _ O _ E _ _ E _

l. _ E _ E _ _ E _

m. F R _ H L _ N G

n. S _ M M _ R

o. H _ R B S T

p. W _ N T _ _

Wunderbar! You've reached the end of Lesson 19. It's time to count up the icons for the exercises and record your result here and in the table on page 128.

Making comparisons

Comparatives & superlatives

The basic rule is that the comparative is formed by adding **-er** to the base form of an adjective or adverb, and the superlative by adding **-ste** (plus the adjective ending where appropriate, i.e. before a noun): **schön** *nice*, **schön**er *nicer*, **schön**ste *nicest*. Some adjectives/adverbs add an umlaut in the comparative and superlative (e.g. **jung, alt, arm, groß, dumm, kalt, warm, lang, kurz**, etc.).

There are three main types of comparisons:

1) comparisons of equality: **so** + adjective/adverb + **wie** *as ... as*:
   Paul ist <u>so</u> groß <u>wie</u> ich. *Paul is as tall as me.*

2) comparisons of inequality: comparative (adj./adv. + **-er**) + **als** *...-er/more than*:
   Paul ist älter **<u>als</u> ich.** *Paul is older than me.* (Note the umlaut.)

   If used before a noun, the comparative declines like an attributive adjective (see p. 120): **Ich nehme die kleiner**e **Tasche.** *I'll take the smaller bag.*

3) comparisons of more than two things (the superlative): definite article + (adj. + **-ste**) *the ...-est*: **Er ist <u>der</u> schnell**ste **Läufer.** *He is the fastest runner.*

   However, the construction **am** + adjective + **-sten** is used for adverbs and predicate adjectives (mainly with verbs other than **sein** *to be*): **<u>Am</u> be**sten **kommst du mit mir.** *It's best to come with me.* **Petra singt <u>am</u> schön**sten. *Petra sings the most beautifully.*

In the table on the right, **klein** is an example of an adjective with regular comparative and superlative forms, **jung** is an example of an adjective that takes an umlaut, and **gern, gut, hoch, nah** and **viel** have irregular comparative and superlative forms.

1	2	3
klein	kleiner	kleinste
jung	jünger	jüngste
gern	lieber	liebste
gut	besser	beste
hoch	höher	höchste
nah	näher	nächste
viel	mehr	meiste

 **Complete the table.**

Comparison of equality	Comparison of inequality	Superlative
.... wie ich.	.... als ich.	Paul ist der dickste/am dicksten von allen.
Sabine ist so schlank wie ich.	.... als ich.	.... von allen.
.... wie ich.	Ana ist schneller als ich.	.... von allen.

2 Put the adjectives/adverbs into the comparative or superlative.

a. Es gibt viele Modelle. Welches möchte er? – Er möchte das .... Modell. **(klein)**

b. Fahren wir mit dem Bus oder dem Zug? – Was ist ....? **(billig)**

c. Der Nil ist mit 6671 Km der .... Fluss der Welt. **(lang)**

d. Mit 828 Metern ist der Burj Khalifa der .... Turm der Welt. **(hoch)**

e. Es gibt einen Zug um 9 Uhr oder um 11 Uhr. Ich nehme den .... Zug. **(früh)**

f. Von uns allen hast du .... gegessen. **(viel)**

Some special cases

- Adjectives ending in **-el**, and some that end in **-er**, normally drop the **e** in the comparative: **edel** *noble* ➜ **edler** *nobler*.

- Adjectives or adverbs ending in **-d**, **-t**, **-s**, **ss**, **-ß**, **-sch** or **-z** usually insert an **e** before the **-ste/-sten** ending in the superlative: **breit** *wide* ➜ **der/die/das breiteste / am breitesten** *the widest*. However, there are some exceptions, e.g. **groß** *big* ➜ **der/die/das größte / am größten** *the biggest* and **spannend** *exciting* ➜ **der/die/das spannendste / am spannendsten** *the most exciting*.

3 Put the adjectives/adverbs into the comparative or superlative.

a. Die Zugfahrt war .... als der Flug. **(teuer)**

b. Sabine ist die .... Schülerin der Klasse. **(hübsch)**

c. Du musst leider .... fahren. **(weit)**

d. Ich nehme die .... Schuhe. **(dunkel)** *(choice between 2 pairs)*

e. Mit 104 Jahren ist sie eine der .... Frauen der Welt. **(alt)**

f. Es ist einer der .... Weißweine. **(süß)**

Expressing likes and preferences

The main verbs for *to like* are **mögen** and **gefallen** (the latter conjugates like *to appeal to*). To express *to like doing something*, the adverb **gern** *gladly, willingly* is used with a verb. Its comparative is **lieber** *more gladly*, and its superlative is **am liebsten** *most gladly*, which are used to express a preference for doing something.

- **gern** + verb *to like doing something*: **Ich esse** gern **spät.** *I like to eat late.*

- **lieber** + verb *to prefer doing something* (a comparison between two things): **Ich trinke** lieber **Bier als Weißwein.** *I prefer drinking beer to white wine.*

- **am liebsten** + verb *to like doing something most/best of all*: Am liebsten **schwimme ich im Meer.** *I like swimming in the sea best.*

Here are some other useful points to keep in mind:

- **gern/lieber/am liebsten** + **haben** can be used to say you like someone. It's chiefly used to express affection in relation to people: **Ich habe Susi gern.** *I like Susi.*

- To say you don't like something, just put **nicht** before **gern** or **lieber**: **Ich trinke nicht gern Bier.** *I don't like drinking beer.* Another option, frequent in everyday speech, is the adverb **ungern** *unwillingly, reluctantly*: **Ich reise ungern.** *I don't like travelling.*

- **gern** + present subjunctive II of **haben** is very commonly used to make a polite request (e.g. in a shop, restaurant, on the phone). This is the equivalent of *would like*: **Ich hätte gern das Schnitzel.** *I'd like* ('would have gladly') *the schnitzel.* **Ich hätte gern Herrn Schmidt.** *I'd like to speak to Mr Schmidt.*

4 Translate the following sentences.

a. I like to go on foot. **(zu Fuß gehen)**

→ ....

b. Do you (**du**) prefer to go by train or by car? **(mit dem Zug / dem Auto fahren)**

→ ....

c. I prefer Ana to Susi.

→ ....

d. Most of all, I like to stay at home.

→ ....

e. I'd like to speak to Mr Müller, please.

→ ....

5 Gern, lieber or am liebsten?

a. Ich gehe......................... ins Kino als ins Theater, aber .... gehe ich ins Ballett.

b. Spielst du Fußball ....?

c. Welches Land in Europa besuchst du ....?

d. Was trinkst du ....? Tee oder Kaffee?

6 Fill in the crossword.

↓ Down
1D popular, in demand
3C to like
5F love
7A to hate

→ Across
1F sweetheart, darling
3J to love
5A darling, treasure

	1	2	3	4	5	6	7	8	9	10
A					S					Z
B							A			
C										
D	B									
E										
F	L							G		
G										
H										
I										
J	T									

'The more/less ... the more/less'

- **Je mehr..., desto** or **umso mehr...** *the more..., the more...*

- **Je weniger..., desto** or **umso weniger...** *the less..., the less...*

These constructions can be used with just a verb: **Je mehr ich esse, desto/ umso mehr möchte ich essen.** *The more I eat, the more I want to eat.*

Or a noun or adjective can be added: **Je mehr Eis er isst, desto/umso weniger Eis haben wir.** *The more ice cream he eats, the less ice cream we have.* **Je weniger ich esse, desto/ umso schlanker bin ich.** *The less I eat, the thinner I am.*

Pay attention to the word order: after **je**, the verb is in the last position, but after **desto** or **umso**, the order is inverted.

7 Complete these sentences with *mehr* or *weniger*.

a. Je mehr du arbeitest, desto/umso .... Zeit hast du.

b. Je mehr Leute du einlädst, desto/umso .... musst du kochen.

c. Je .... Geld du verdienst, umso mehr gibst du aus.

d. Je mehr du heute arbeitest, desto/umso .... musst du morgen arbeiten.

'What kind/sort of...?'

This question is formed with **Was für ein(e)...?** (singular – **ein(e)** declines) or **Was für...?** (plural). Be careful, because in this context **für** is not a preposition, so the case of the following noun phrase depends on its function in the sentence and not on **für** (which as a preposition takes the accusative):

Was für <u>ein Wagen</u> ist das? *What kind of car is that?* (noun phrase in the masc. nominative as **Wagen** is the subject)

<u>Mit</u> was für <u>einem Wagen</u> seid ihr gefahren? *What kind of car did you drive here in?* (noun phrase in the masc. dative as **mit** takes the dative case)

Was für Wagen sind das? *What kinds of cars are those?* (in the plural, there is no article)

8 Form the questions using *was für*.

E.g. Ich mag alte Filme.
→ Was für Filme magst du gern?

a. Ich habe ein kleines Auto.

→ ....

b. Ich lese gern Geschichtsbücher.

→ ....

c. Ich bin mit einer kleinen Maschine geflogen.

→ ....

d. Ich gehe lieber in ein typisches Restaurant.

→ ....

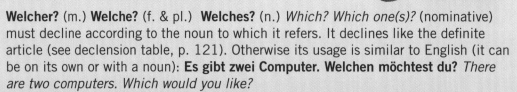

'Which...? / Which one(s)...?'

Welcher? (m.) **Welche?** (f. & pl.) **Welches?** (n.) *Which? Which one(s)?* (nominative) must decline according to the noun to which it refers. It declines like the definite article (see declension table, p. 121). Otherwise its usage is similar to English (it can be on its own or with a noun): **Es gibt zwei Computer. Welchen möchtest du?** *There are two computers. Which would you like?*

Welch- may be preceded by a preposition (in spoken English, the preposition is usually at the end of the sentence, but in German it comes at the beginning): **Mit welchem Computer arbeitest du?** *Which computer are you working on?*

Note that **welch-** is practically never used in the genitive.

9 Form questions with *welch-* following the example.
E.g. Ich kenne den jüngeren Sohn. → Welchen (Sohn) kennst du?

a. Ich nehme meistens die Linie *(route)* 5. → ....

b. Ich war auf der deutschen Schule. → ....

c. Ich lese oft die Süddeutsche Zeitung. → ....

d. Ich gehe oft zum Bäcker in der Wilhelmstraße. → ....

Translate these sentences.

a. Which newspaper do you (**du**) work for? → ....

b. Which teacher *(m.)* are you (**du**) learning German with? → ....

c. Which company (**die Firma**) does he work in? → ....

d. I don't know which train he took. → ....

e. Which books are for me? → ....

Finally, while we're at it, let's take the opportunity to review a few adjectives.

 Find the opposites of:

schnell – sauer – böse – trocken – glücklich – dick – leicht – leise

a. lieb ≠ ....

b. langsam ≠ ....

c. schlank ≠ ....

d. nass ≠ ....

e. laut ≠ ....

f. süß ≠ ....

g. traurig ≠ ....

h. schwer ≠ ....

On which adjectives are these nouns based?

a. die Gesundheit / die Krankheit

→ ....

b. die Stärke / die Schwäche

→ ....

c. der Fleiß / die Faulheit

→ ....

d. die Intelligenz / die Dummheit

→ ....

Well done! You've reached the end of Lesson 20. It's time to count up the icons for the exercises and record your result here and in the table on page 128.

Numbers

Cardinal numbers

0 null	21 einundzwanzig
1 eins	22 zweiundzwanzig
2 zwei	30 dreißig
3 drei	40 vierzig
4 vier	50 fünfzig
5 fünf	60 sechzig
6 sechs	70 siebzig
7 sieben	80 achtzig
8 acht	90 neunzig
9 neun	100 (ein)hundert
10 zehn	101 einhunderteins
11 elf	200 zweihundert
12 zwölf	350 dreihundertfünfzig
13 dreizehn	1,000 (ein)tausend
14 vierzehn	1,500 tausendfünfhundert
15 fünfzehn	10,000 zehntausend
16 sechzehn	100,000 hunderttausend
17 siebzehn	1,000,000 eine Million
18 achtzehn	1,000,100,000 eine Milliard
19 neunzehn	hunderttausend
20 zwanzig	

Note that German numbers from 21 to 99 are formed 'backwards', with the smaller number first: *21* 'one-and-twenty'. Numbers are written as one word up to 999,999. A decimal point is written as a **Komma**, whereas a point or space is used as a thousands separator.

Ordinal numbers

- 1st to 19th: These are formed by adding the suffix **t** + adjective ending, e.g. **2.** *2nd* (**der zweite**), **4.** *4th* (**der vierte**), **19.** *19th* (**der neunzehnte**). (Note that a period written after the number indicates that it is ordinal.) There are a few irregular forms: **1.** (**der erste**), **3.** (**der dritte**), **7.** (**der siebte**) and **8.** (**der achte**).

- 20th upwards: These are formed by adding the suffix **st** + adjective ending, e.g. **20.** (**der zwanzigste**), **45.** (**der fünfundvierzigste**), **1000.** (**der tausendste**), etc.

Ordinals are used for dates, centuries, royal titles, etc. ➜ **Ludwig XIV.** = **Ludwig der Vierzehnte.**

---

1 Write these numbers as words. ˙˙

a. 17,25

→ ....

b. 860

→ ....

c. 1.400 000

→ ....

2 Write the below as words. ˙˙

a. zum 10. Mal

→ ....

b. im 21.Jahrhundert

→ ....

c. Papst Paul VI.

→ ....

The date

- There are several ways to ask **das Datum** *the date*; note that it is always given using an ordinal number: **Welcher Tag / Der Wievielte ist heute? Heute ist Montag, der 2. Mai.** (nominative) **Welchen Tag / Den Wievielten haben wir heute? Heute haben wir Montag, den 2. Mai.** (accusative)

- To specify the date of an event, you use the preposition **am**: **Er ist am 3. Mai geboren.** *He was born on the 3rd of May.* And to specify the day, you use the preposition **am** followed by **den** or **dem** (both are grammatically correct): **Er ist am Montag, den/dem 3. Mai geboren.** *He was born on Monday, the 3rd of May.*

- To give the month or the season, use the preposition **im**: **Es war im Juli / im Sommer.** *It was in July / in the summer.*

- To give the year, you can just give the number (e.g. **zweitausendsechzehn**) or else **im Jahr 2016**; the anglicism **in 2016** is increasingly common.

- For holidays, the preposition can be either **an** or **zu**: **Wo seid ihr an/zu Ostern?** *Where will you be at Easter?*

2016

3 Fill in the days of the week.

a. M _ _ _ _ _

b. D _ _ _ _ _ _ _

c. M _ _ _ _ _ _

d. D _ _ _ _ _ _ _ _ _

e. F _ _ _ _ _ _

f. S _ _ _ _ _ _

g. S _ _ _ _ _ _

4 Answer the questions with the dates indicated written out as words.

a. Wann bist du angekommen? **(16. Juli)**

→ ....

b. Was für ein Datum ist heute? **(29. Februar)**

→ ....

c. Wann warst du in Berlin? **(Mai 2012)**

→ ....

d. Wann haben sie geheiratet? **(Samstag, 15. Mai)**

→ ....

e. Wann fahrt ihr weg? **(Weihnachten)**

→ ....

Glückwunsch! You've now completed all of the exercises in this workbook! It's time to count up the icons for Lesson 21 and record your result here and in the final table on page 128.

Verb conjugation tables

INDICATIVE

IMPERATIVE

Auxiliary verbs (*sein*, *haben*, *werden*), weak verbs (*lernen*) and strong verbs (*fahren*)

	Present		Simple past		Present perfect		Future		Imperative	
SEIN	bin	sind	war	waren	bin gewesen	sind gewesen	werde sein	werden sein	Sei!	Seid!
	bist	seid	warst	wart	bist gewesen	seid gewesen	wirst sein	werdet sein	Seien wir!	Seien Sie!
	ist	sind	war	waren	ist gewesen	sind gewesen	wird sein	werden sein		
HABEN	habe	haben	hatte	hatten	habe gehabt	haben gehabt	werde haben	werden haben	Hab(e)!	Habt!
	hast	habt	hattest	hattet	hast gehabt	habt gehabt	wirst haben	werdet haben	Haben wir!	Haben Sie!
	hat	haben	hatte	hatten	hat gehabt	haben gehabt	wird haben	werden haben		
WERDEN	werde	werden	wurde	wurden	bin geworden	sind geworden	werde werden	werden werden	Werde!	Werdet!
	wirst	werdet	wurdest	wurdet	bist geworden	seid geworden	wirst werden	werdet werden	Werden wir!	Werden Sie!
	wird	werden	wurde	wurden	ist geworden	sind geworden	wird werden	werden werden		
LERNEN	lerne	lernen	lernte	lernten	habe gelernt	haben gelernt	werde lernen	werden lernen	Lern(e)	Lernt!
	lernst	lernt	lerntest	lerntet	hast gelernt	habt gelernt	wirst lernen	werdet lernen	Lernen wir!	Lernen Sie!
	lernt	lernen	lernte	lernten	hat gelernt	haben gelernt	wird lernen	werden lernen		
FAHREN	fahre	fahren	fuhr	fuhren	bin gefahren	sind gefahren	werde fahren	werden fahren	Fahr(e)!	Fahrt!
	fährst	fahrt	fuhrst	fuhrt	bist gefahren	seid gefahren	wirst fahren	werdet fahren	Fahren wir!	Fahren Sie!
	fährt	fahren	fuhr	fuhren	ist gefahren	sind gefahren	wird fahren	werden fahren		

Modal verbs – present tense

mögen		können		müssen		dürfen		wollen		sollen		wissen	
mag	mögen	kann	können	muss	müssen	darf	dürfen	will	wollen	soll	sollen	weiß	wissen
magst	mögt	kannst	könnt	musst	müsst	darfst	dürft	willst	wollt	sollst	sollt	weißt	wisst
mag	mögen	kann	können	muss	müssen	darf	dürfen	will	wollen	soll	sollen	weiß	wissen

Modal verbs – simple past (preterite)

mögen		können		müssen		dürfen		wollen		sollen		wissen	
mochte	mochten	konnte	konnten	musste	mussten	durfte	durften	wollte	wollten	sollte	sollten	wusste	wussten
mochtest	mochtet	konntest	konntet	musstest	musstet	durftest	durftet	wolltest	wolltet	solltest	solltet	wusstest	wusstet
mochte	mochten	konnte	konnten	musste	mussten	durfte	durften	wollte	wollten	sollte	sollten	wusste	wussten

Modal verbs – past participles

mögen	können	müssen	dürfen	wollen	sollen	wissen
gemocht	gekonnt	gemusst	gedurft	gewollt	gesollt	gewusst

.../...

Irregular weak verbs – simple past (preterite)

bringen	brennen	denken	kennen	nennen	rennen	senden	wenden
brachte	brannte	dachte	kannte	nannte	rannte	sandte/sendete	wandte/wendete

… / …

Irregular weak verbs – past participles

bringen	brennen	denken	kennen	nennen	senden	wenden
gebracht	gebrannt	gedacht	gekannt	genannt	gesandt/gesendet	gewandt/gewendet

… / …

SUBJUNCTIVE

Subjunctive II – future

kommen	
würde kommen	würden kommen
würdest kommen	würdet kommen
würde kommen	würden kommen

Subjunctive II – past (contrary-to-fact)

kommen	lernen
wäre gekommen	hätte gelernt
wär(e)st gekommen	hättest gelernt
wäre gekommen	hätte gelernt
wären gekommen	hätten gelernt
wär(e)t gekommen	hättet gelernt
wären gekommen	hätten gelernt

Subjunctive II – present (used mainly with *sein*, *haben* and the modal verbs)

sein		haben		mögen		können		müssen	
wäre	wären	hätte	hätten	möchte	möchten	könnte	könnten	müsste	müssten
wär(e)st	wär(e)t	hättest	hättet	möchtest	möchtet	könntest	könntet	müsstest	müsstet
wäre	wären	hätte	hätten	möchte	möchten	könnte	könnten	müsste	müssten

dürfen		wollen		sollen		wissen	
dürfte	dürften	wollte	wollten	sollte	sollten	wüsste	wüssten
dürftest	dürftet	wolltest	wolltet	solltest	solltet	wüsstest	wüsstet
dürfte	dürften	wollte	wollten	sollte	sollten	wüsste	wüssten

PASSIVE

	Present	Simple past	Present perfect
einladen	werde eingeladen	wurde eingeladen	bin eingeladen worden
	wirst eingeladen	wurdest eingeladen	bist eingeladen worden
	wird eingeladen	wurde eingeladen	ist eingeladen worden
	werden eingeladen	wurden eingeladen	sind eingeladen worden
	werdet eingeladen	wurdet eingeladen	seid eingeladen worden
	werden eingeladen	wurden eingeladen	sind eingeladen worden

Declension tables

Weak declension (type I): attributive adjective preceded by a definite article or demonstrative

	Masculine		Feminine		Neuter		Plural	
Nominative	der dieser	gute Wein	die diese	gute Limonade	das dieses	gute Bier	die diese	guten Weine
Accusative	den diesen	guten Wein	die diese	gute Limonade	das dieses	gute Bier	die diese	guten Weine
Dative	dem diesem	guten Wein	der dieser	guten Limonade	dem diesem	guten Bier	den diesen	guten Weinen
Genitive	des dieses	guten Weins	der dieser	guten Limonade	des dieses	guten Biers	der dieser	guten Weine

Strong declension (type II): attributive adjective unpreceded by an article, demonstrative, etc.

	Masculine	Feminine	Neuter	Plural
Nominative	guter Wein	gute Limonade	gutes Bier	gute Weine
Accusative	guten Wein	gute Limonade	gutes Bier	gute Weine
Dative	gutem Wein	guter Limonade	gutem Bier	guten Weinen
Genitive	guten Weins	guter Limonade	guten Biers	guter Weine

Mixed declension (type III): attributive adjective preceded by an indefinite article or possessive

	Masculine		Feminine		Neuter		Plural
Nominative	ein mein	guter Wein	eine meine	gute Limonade	ein mein	gutes Bier	— * meine guten Weine
Accusative	einen meinen	guten Wein	eine meine	gute Limonade	ein mein	gutes Bier	— * meine guten Weine
Dative	einem meinem	guten Wein	einer meiner	guten Limonade	einem meinem	guten Bier	— * meinen guten Weinen
Genitive	eines meines	guten Weins	einer meiner	guten Limonade	eines meines	guten Biers	— * meiner guten Weine

*Because there is no plural indefinite article, this follows the pattern of a strong declension (type II) plural: **gute Weine, gute Limonaden**, etc.

Personal pronouns

Nominative	ich	du	er	sie	es	wir	ihr	sie	Sie
Accusative	mich	dich	ihn	sie	es	uns	euch	sie	Sie
Dative	mir	dir	ihm	ihr	ihm	uns	euch	ihnen	Ihnen

Reflexive pronouns

Nominative	ich	du	er	sie	es	wir	ihr	sie	Sie
Accusative	mich	dich	sich	sich	sich	uns	euch	sich	sich
Dative	mir	dir	sich	sich	sich	uns	euch	sich	sich

Possessive adjectives (nominative)

	Masc.	Feminine	Neuter	Plural
my	mein	meine	mein	meine
your (inf.)	dein	deine	dein	deine
his, its	sein	seine	sein	seine
her, its	ihr	ihre	ihr	ihre
our	unser	unsere	unser	unsere
your (pl.)	euer	eure	euer	eure
their	ihr	ihre	ihr	ihre
Formal your	Ihr	Ihre	Ihr	Ihre

Possessive pronouns (nominative)

	Masc.	Feminine	Neuter	Plural
mine	meiner	meine	mein(e)s	meine
yours (inf.)	deiner	deine	dein(e)s	deine
his	seiner	seine	sein(e)s	seine
hers	ihrer	ihre	ihr(e)s	ihre
ours	uns(e)rer	uns(e)re	uns(e)res	uns(e)re
yours (pl.)	eu(e)rer	eu(e)re	eu(e)res	eu(e)re
theirs	ihrer	ihre	ihres	ihre
Formal yours	Ihrer	Ihre	Ihres	Ihre

Interrogative pronouns and adjectives

	Who(m)/Whose?	What?
Nominative	wer	was
Accusative	wen	was
Dative	wem	— *
Genitive	wessen	— *

Which?/Which ones?			
Masculine	Feminine	Neuter	Plural
welcher	welche	welches	welche
welchen	welche	welches	welche
welchem	welcher	welchem	welchen
—	—	—	—

* **Was** is mainly used in the nominative and accusative.
For the other cases, the form **wo(r)** + preposition is used.

Indefinite pronouns

	Masculine	Feminine	Neuter	Plural
Nominative	einer / keiner	eine / keine	ein(e)s / kein(e)s*	– / keine
Accusative	einen / keinen	eine / keine	ein(e)s / kein(e)s*	– / keine
Dative	einem / keinem	einer / keiner	einem / keinem	– / keinen

* The **e** is optional; it is usually omitted.

Relative & demonstrative pronouns

	Masculine	Feminine	Neuter	Plural
Nominative	der	die	das	die
Accusative	den	die	das	die
Dative	dem	der	dem	denen
Genitive	dessen	deren	dessen	deren

ANSWERS

1. The present tense

1 **wohnen:** wohne, wohnst, wohnt, wohnen, wohnt, wohnen **beginnen:** beginne, beginnst, beginnt, beginnen, beginnt, beginnen **fragen:** frage, fragst, fragt, fragen, fragt, fragen **fahren:** fahre, fährst, fährt, fahren, fahrt, fahren **laufen:** laufe, läufst, läuft, laufen, lauft, laufen **nehmen:** nehme, nimmst, nimmt, nehmen, nehmt, nehmen

2 **a.** (IR) er/sie/es sieht **b.** (R) **c.** (IR) er/sie/es schläft **d.** (IR) er/sie/es fällt **e.** (R) **f.** (R) **g.** (R) **h.** (IR) er/sie/es trifft

3 **Line 1:** bin, bist, ist, sind, seid, sind **Line 2:** habe, hast, hat, haben, habt, haben **Line 3:** werde, wirst, wird, werden, werdet, werden

4 **a.** finde **b.** lesen **c.** bitte **d.** spricht **e.** grüßt **f.** empfiehlst

5 **a.** sprechen → er/sie/es spricht **b.** schreiben → er/sie/es schreibt **c.** trinken → er/sie/es trinkt **d.** lieben → er/sie/es liebt **e.** fliegen → er/sie/es fliegt **f.** reparieren → er/sie/es repariert

6 **baden:** bade, badest, badet, baden, badet, baden **reisen:** reise, reist, reist, reisen, reist, reisen **wechseln:** wechs(e)le, wechselst, wechselt, wechseln, wechselt, wechseln

7 **a.** ihr antwortet **b.** er/sie/es zeichnet **c.** sie verändern **d.** du liest

8 **a.** Haben Sie Zeit? **b.** Hast du Zeit? **c.** Habt ihr Zeit? **d.** Haben sie Zeit?

9 **Line 1:** Hallo, wer seid ihr? / Guten Tag, wer sind Sie? **Line 2:** Wie heißt ihr? – Paul und Sabine, und ihr? / Wie heißen Sie? – Paul (und Sabine), und Sie? **Line 3:** Woher kommt ihr? / Woher kommen Sie? **Line 4:** Wo wohnt ihr? / Wo wohnen Sie? **Line 5:** Wie lange seid ihr schon in Berlin? / Wie lange sind Sie schon in Berlin? **Line 6:** Schön, dass ihr gekommen seid. / Schön, dass Sie gekommen sind. **Line 7:** Tschüss! / Auf Wiedersehen!

10 **a.** bald **b.** morgen **c.** später **d.** Nacht **e.** gleich

11 **a.** Und ihr? **b.** Mich auch! **c.** Dir nicht? **d.** Du auch? **e.** Und Ihnen?

2. The imperative

1 **a.** Kommt! **b.** Sing(e) nicht zu laut! **c.** Rufen wir an! **d.** Lest das Buch! **e.** Gehen wir spazieren! **f.** Bleiben Sie da! **g.** Kommt mit! **h.** Kauf(e) Blumen!

2 **a.** Sei bitte pünktlich! **b.** Seien wir ehrlich! **c.** Seid nett zu ihr! **d.** Seien Sie nicht traurig! **e.** Sei vorsichtig!

3 1f – 2e – 3c – 4d – 5b – 6a – 7g

4 1b (aus) 2e (rückwärts) 3d (runter) 4a (weniger) 5c (zu)

5 **Line 1:** Arbeite schneller! **Line 2:** Verändert nichts! **Line 3:** Badet nicht jetzt! **Line 4:** Ärgere mich nicht! **Line 5:** Wechs(e)le 100 Euro! **Line 6:** Ladet ihn ein!

6 **a.** Find(e) / Findet **b.** Schreib(e) / Schreibt **c.** Lass(e) / Lasst **d.** Schneid(e) / Schneidet **e.** Steig(e) / Steigt **f.** Hab(e) / Habt

7 1g – 2a – 3f – 4b – 5d – 6e – 7c

8 1g – 2a – 3b – 4f – 5c – 6d – 7e

9 **a.** Ruhe! **b.** Achtung! **c.** Raus! **d.** Los!

10 **a.** Wald **b.** Baum **c.** Blatt **d.** Blume **e.** Meer **f.** beach **g.** Sand **h.** wave **i.** Berg **j.** stream **k.** grass **l.** stone **m.** farm **n.** Tier **o.** stable **p.** field

11 1c – 2f – 3e – 4b – 5a – 6d

12 **a.** der Löwe **b.** die Katze **c.** das Schwein **d.** das Schaf **e.** der Schmetterling **f.** die Mücke **g.** der Vogel **h.** die Maus **i.** die Kuh **j.** der Wolf **k.** die Giraffe **l.** die Ameise **m.** das Pferd **n.** der Hase **o.** der Fisch **p.** die Biene **q.** die Spinne **r.** die Wespe

13 **a.** bellen **b.** miauen **c.** schwimmen **d.** fliegen **e.** brüllen **f.** stechen

14 **a.** To have a frog in one's throat **b.** To be hungry enough to eat a horse **c.** To stick out like a sore thumb **d.** To kill two birds with one stone

3. The present perfect

1 **a.** gesucht **b.** gekauft **c.** gepackt **d.** geduscht **e.** gehört

2 **a.** gesehen **b.** getrunken **c.** gefunden **d.** gelaufen **e.** genommen **f.** springen **g.** helfen **h.** essen **i.** bleiben **j.** gehen

3 **a.** telefoniert **b.** abgeschickt **c.** eingeladen **d.** angekommen **e.** versucht **f.** gehört **g.** verboten **h.** repariert

4 **a.** habe **b.** sind **c.** haben **d.** seid **e.** hat **f.** hat

5 **a.** Er hat viel getrunken. **b.** Er ist schnell gelaufen. **c.** Er hat sich gewaschen. **d.** Es hat geschneit. **e.** Er ist bei mir gewesen. **f.** Er ist gekommen.

6 **a.** Ich habe kein neues Auto. **b.** Sie ist nicht zu schnell gefahren. **c.** Ich habe keine Arbeit. **d.** Ich liebe dich nicht. **e.** Das ist kein Gold. **f.** Ich denke nicht an die Arbeit.

7 1g – 2e – 3f – 4a – 5d – 6b – 7c

8 geboren / gemacht / gegangen / gelernt / gegeben / gewesen / studiert / gemacht / kennen gelernt

9 1. Schmitt 2. Robert 3. 5.09.1982 4. Köln 5. deutsch 6. verheiratet 7. Medizin 8. Kinderarzt 9. Deutsch, Englisch, Spanisch, Portugiesisch 10. Sprachen, Reisen

10 **a.** eye colour **b.** sex **c.** expiration date **d.** address **e.** holder's signature **f.** height

11

T	M	A	L	E	N	P	S
U	U	T	O	A	O	F	P
K	S	A	K	S	T	G	O
M	I	N	O	H	E	V	R
B	K	Z	C	I	S	E	T
V	U	E	H	U	A	S	E
O	K	N	E	K	L	A	R
I	S	I	N	G	E	N	U
H	C	E	R	I	S	U	T
R	H	H	S	M	E	I	D
E	A	N	K	I	N	O	D
B	C	M	V	L	H	O	S
B	H	L	M	K	U	L	V

music: Musik
to draw/to paint: malen
sport: Sport
to cook: kochen
cinema: Kino
to dance: tanzen
chess: Schach
to sing: singen
to read: lesen

4. The simple past

1 **Line 1:** baute, bautest, baute, bauten, bautet, bauten **Line 2:** sagte, sagtest, sagte, sagten, sagtet, sagten

2 **Line 1:** lief, liefst, lief, liefen, lieft, liefen **Line 2:** log, logst, log, logen, logt, logen

3 **Infinitive:** tragen, helfen, schreiben, geben **First-person singular simple past:** nahm, ging, las, flog

4 **Line 1:** war, warst, war, waren, wart, waren **Line 2:** hatte, hattest, hatte, hatten, hattet, hatten **Line 3:** wurde, wurdest, wurde, wurden, wurdet, wurden

5. a. fandet **b.** zeichnetest **c.** last **d.** redeten

6. a. landen → to land **b.** beten → to pray **c.** raten → to advise **d.** (sich) streiten → to quarrel **e.** bitten → to request, ask for **f.** empfinden → to feel, sense

7. a. kennt **b.** brennt **c.** nennen **d.** rennt **e.** denke

8. a. brannte → gebrannt **b.** brachte → gebracht **c.** dachte → gedacht **d.** kannte → gekannt **e.** nannte → genannt

9. a. Wenn **b.** wenn **c.** wann **d.** Als

10. a. When he was born, **b.** When he was 20 years old, **c.** When he passed his school-leaving exam, **d.** When he married, **e.** When he had his first child, **f.** When he died,

11. a. Viertel vor sechs / fünf Uhr fünfundvierzig **b.** zehn nach acht / acht Uhr zehn **c.** halb drei / vierzehn Uhr dreißig **d.** Viertel nach fünf / siebzehn Uhr fünfzehn **e.** fünf nach acht / acht Uhr fünf **f.** zehn nach drei / fünfzehn Uhr zehn

12. a. um **b.** gegen **c.** am **d.** am **e.** am **f.** am **g.** am **h.** in der **i.** Um wie viel Uhr?

13. a. heute Abend **b.** morgen Nachmittag **c.** gestern Morgen **d.** heute Nachmittag

14.
```
          U       A
          H       U
    W E C K E R   F
      E   L       W
  W A C H   M     A
      K   N I     C
      E   G N     H
      N   S E K U N D E
          L   T   N
  Z     S T U N D E
  E     C
  E I N S C H L A F E N
  T     L
        A
        F
```

5. The future

1. a. Du wirst nach Berlin fliegen. **b.** Wir werden dir helfen. **c.** Er wird anrufen. **d.** Sie werden einen Brief bekommen.

2. a. Morgen schreibt sie dir eine Mail. **b.** Am Dienstag machen sie das. **c.** Am Wochenende schneit es.

3. a. hell / dunkel **b.** Elektriker **c.** spät **d.** Zeit **e.** gelb

4. a. Vor dem Essen gehe ich ins Schwimmbad. **b.** correct **c.** Wenn der Film bis 22 Uhr dauert, gehe ich lieber davor etwas essen. **d.** Essen wir vor oder nach dem Film?

5. a. gemacht habe **b.** gelebt hatte **c.** ging **d.** putze

6. a. craftsman **b.** policeman **c.** lawyer **d.** computer scientist **e.** fireman **f.** gardener **g.** actor **h.** mechanic **i.** doctor **j.** nurse **k.** hairdresser **l.** insurance agent

7. a. die Köchin **b.** die Sängerin **c.** die Musikerin **d.** die Bäckerin **e.** die Verkäuferin **f.** die Tänzerin **g.** die Lehrerin **h.** die Putzfrau

8. a. Arzt/Ärztin, Krankenpfleger/Krankenschwester **b.** Lehrer/Lehrerin **c.** Musiker/Musikerin **d.** Koch/Köchin **e.** Mechaniker/Mechanikerin, Handwerker/Handwerkerin **f.** Rechtsanwalt/Rechtsanwältin **g.** Arzt/Ärztin, Krankenpfleger/Krankenschwester **h.** Verkäufer/ Verkäuferin **i.** Bäcker/ Bäckerin **j.** Fischer/Fischerin

9. a. Tomorrow is another day. (It can wait until tomorrow.) **b.** Never put off until tomorrow what can be done today. **c.** The early bird catches the worm.

6. The subjunctive II

1. a. ich würde schlafen **b.** er würde lernen **c.** ihr würdet gehen **d.** du würdest anrufen **e.** wir würden lesen **f.** Sie würden warten

2. a. wir wüssten **b.** du könntest **c.** ihr wolltet **d.** sie wären **e.** du dürftest **f.** er müsste **g.** ihr wüsstet **h.** ich wäre **i.** Sie hätten

3. a. ich wäre gekommen **b.** wir wären geblieben **c.** du hättest gesagt **d.** ihr hättet gefragt **e.** er hätte geschrieben **f.** Sie wären gegangen

4. a. hätte **b.** gewesen wären **c.** hast **d.** geregnet hätte **e.** könnte **f.** lieben würdest

5. 1d – 2e – 3b – 4a – 5c

6. a. ob **b.** Wenn **c.** ob **d.** wenn **e.** Ob **f.** ob **g.** ob / wenn

7. 1a – 2b / 3c – 4d / 5f – 6e / 7g – 8h / 9j – 10i / 11l – 12k / 13n – 14m

8. a. Hose **b.** Hemd **c.** Rock **d.** Mantel **e.** Kleid **f.** Jacke **g.** Pulli **h.** Schuhe **i.** Hut **j.** Unterhose **k.** Strümpfe **l.** Strumpfhose

9. a. Größe **b.** Farbe **c.** anprobieren **d.** klein / kurz **e.** groß / lang **f.** Paar **g.** passt

10.
```
  G R A U
  O               O
S C H W A R Z
A       E       A
        I       N
      B           B
      G E L B       R O T
      R     L I L A
      Ü     A       U
      N     U       N
```

11. a. Handtasche → handbag **b.** Gürtel → belt **c.** Hosenträger → braces/suspenders **d.** Geldbeutel → wallet **e.** Taschentuch → handkerchief **f.** Regenschirm → umbrella **g.** Sonnenbrille → sunglasses

7. The passive voice

1. a. Der Rasen ist vom Gärtner gemäht worden. **b.** Die Maschinen werden oft von den Technikern kontrolliert. **c.** Der Brief wurde von der Sekretärin geschrieben. **d.** 1906 malte Picasso dieses Bild. **e.** Wer komponierte die Zauberflöte? **f.** Eine Wespe hat mich gestochen. **g.** Die Geschenke werden von den Kindern eingepackt. **h.** Mein Vater baute das Haus.

2. a. Um 21 Uhr ist das Geschäft geschlossen. **b.** Um 13 Uhr ist das Essen gekocht. **c.** Am Abend war alles vorbereitet. **d.** Für die Feier war das ganze Haus geputzt.

3. a. Das Auto ist repariert worden. **b.** Es wird viel getanzt. **c.** Die Fassade wird renoviert. **d.** Damals wurden Briefe geschrieben. **e.** Im Sommer wurde später gegessen. **f.** Ich bin zum Essen eingeladen worden.

4. a. gefunden **b.** empfangen **c.** bestellt **d.** angehalten **e.** untersucht **f.** unterbrochen

5. a. angeschaut **b.** angesehen / angeschaut **c.** ansehen / anschauen **d.** sehen **e.** geschaut

6. a. Nachspeise **b.** Fleisch / Gemüse **c.** Getränke **d.** Kuchen / Obstsalat **e.** Rechnung / Trinkgeld

7. 1b – 2d – 3e – 4c – 5a

8 Kartoffel / Karotte / Salat / Bohne / Gemüse / Apfel / Tomate / Orange / Erdbeeren / Früchte, Obst

9 Tisch / Personen / Uhr / Uhr / Namen / Terrasse / frei / voll / Uhr / Tisch / drinnen / Name

10

					S	A	L	Z		
					E					
	T	E	L	L	E	R				
			ö		R		V			
			F				I			
	G		P	F	E	F	F	E	R	
	L		E				T			
G	A	B	E	L			T			
	S					M	E	S	S	E	R

11 1d – 2a – 3b – 4c – 5f – 6e

8. Nouns & the nominative

1 a. Dieser kleine Junge b. ein schönes Instrument c. Diese alte Dame d. Weiße Schuhe e. Dieser junge Mann

2 a. das Paket → Was ist für Paul? b. Paul → Wer sucht den Hausschlüssel? c. der Ausweis → Was liegt hier? d. Sie → Wer ist die neue Deutschlehrerin? / die neue Deutschlehrerin → Wer ist sie?

3 a. die b. die c. das d. die e. das f. der g. das h. die i. der j. der k. das l. die m. die n. das o. das p. das

4 a. die Lehrerin b. der Freund c. das Mädchen d. die Mutter e. der Verkäufer f. der Arzt g. die Bäuerin h. die Schwester

5 a. die Wagen b. die Blumen c. die Sängerinnen d. die Fotos e. die Stühle f. die Vögel

6 a. das Buch b. die Frucht c. der Tisch d. der Gott e. das Heft f. das Büro

7 1b – 2a / 3d – 4c / 5e – 6f / 7h – 8g

8 a. der Onkel b. das Mädchen c. die Übung d. das Essen e. das Instrument f. der Strauß g. der Tag h. der Eingang

9 a. der Badeanzug b. der Bademeister c. die Badehose d. das Badetuch e. der Sommerurlaub f. die Sommernacht g. die Sommersprossen h. das Sommerkleid i. der Sonnenstich j. der Sonnenschirm k. die Sonnenkreme l. der Sonnenbrand

10 1d Eingangstür 2h not a compound 3f Schlafzimmer 4b Badezimmer 5c Wohnzimmer 6e Esszimmer 7g Briefkasten 8a Kinderzimmer

11 a. der Esstisch b. der Schreibtisch c. das Kinderbett d. der Kleiderschrank e. – f. – g. – h. die Spülmaschine i. die Waschmaschine j. der Kühlschrank k. – l. das Bücherregal

12 a. geklopft b. geklingelt c. aufmachen d. herein e. Platz f. anbieten g. Besuch

13

W	N	M	K	O	U	J	I	S
A	S	K	M	C	A	V	K	P
S	X	L	L	T	S	X	O	I
C	T	O	I	L	E	T	T	E
H	C	R	K	L	H	W	N	G
B	A	D	E	W	A	N	N	E
E	Z	U	D	F	E	E	B	L
C	L	S	S	X	C	X	A	P
K	L	C	A	F	K	D	A	M
E	H	H	Y	O	E	F	E	J
N	N	E	I	U	N	O	D	B
R	D	V	P	G	R	U	C	V

bathtub: Badewanne
sink: Waschbecken
mirror: Spiegel
shower: Dusche
toilets: Toilette or Klo

14 Hausnummer / Postleitzahl / Hausmeister / Adresse / Telefonnummer / Hausschlüssel / Anschrift

9. The accusative

1 a. diesen jungen Schauspieler b. dieses neue Theaterstück c. diese russische Tänzerin d. diese französischen Filme

2 a. frische Brötchen b. die neue Schulreform c. einen kleinen Test d. kein schöner Film e. ein kleines Hotel f. der Briefträger

3 a. sie b. ihn c. euch d. dich

4 a. keine b. ein(e)s c. keiner d. ein(e)s

5 a. diesen Samstag b. die ganze Woche c. Nächsten Monat d. ein ganzes Jahr e. Letztes Mal

6 a. viel b. sehr c. Viele d. viel e. vielen f. sehr g. sehr

7 a. Du trinkst viel. b. Er trinkt viel Wasser. c. Es gibt viele Leute. d. Er liebt dich sehr. e. Es ist sehr schön. f. Sie hat sehr viel Geld.

8 a. Have fun! b. Good luck! ('Much success!') c. Good luck! d. Enjoy yourself! e. Thanks very much! f. With pleasure! ('Very gladly!') g. Dear Sir …

9 1c – 2e – 3f – 4a – 5b – 6d

10 a. alt b. lang / breit c. schwer d. hoch e. weit

11 a. breit b. lang c. alt d. schnell e. schwer f. groß

12 a. gewicht b. alter c. geschwindigkeit d. höhe e. länge

13

				W			
				O			
		W		W		H	
W	I	E		A		I	
		E		WESSEN
		S		A			
W	O	H	E	R			
		E		U			
		R	W	E	M		
				E			
W	A	N	N				
I							
W	I	E		L	A	N	G	E
V							
W	I	E		O	F	T	
E							
L							

10. The dative

1 a. einer kleinen Stadt b. den Kindern c. dem Bruder d. dieser Dame e. einem alten Mann f. diesem Mann g. einem Monat

2 a. mir b. ihr c. Ihnen d. dir e. uns

3 a. einer einzigen Schülerin b. kleinen Kindern c. einem armen Mann d. einer alten Dame

4 1c – 2f – 3e – 4b – 5a – 6d

5 a. Ich habe euch ein Päckchen geschickt. b. Ich schenke dir die Uhr. c. Ich habe es ihr gesagt. d. Ich habe deinem Bruder das Geld gegeben.

6 a. Ich habe ihr eine Mail geschrieben. b. Ich habe sie Paul geschrieben. c. Wir schenken es ihnen.

7 a. Er hat zu viel Arbeit. b. Es ist zu weit. c. Ich sehe sie wenig. d. Er schläft zu wenig. e. Er ärgert mich zu sehr. f. Er macht zu wenig Sport.

8 1d – 2e – 3b – 4f – 5c – 6g – 7a

⑨ Fig. 1: ② Ohr ③ Auge ⑥ Kinn ⑤ Mund ① Stirn ④ Nase ⑧ Schulter ⑦ Hals **Fig. 2:** ① Kopf ③ Arm ⑤ Hand ⑦ Bein ⑥ Finger ⑧ Knie ④ Bauch ⑨ Fuß ② Brust ⑩ Zeh

⑩

			M									
			E									
			D									
	S	E	I			G						
C	R		I									
H	K	R	A	N	K	H	E	I	T			
M	Ä	P	A		S							
E	L	O	M		U					K		
A	R	Z	T		T	E		N		R		
Z	U	H	N		D			D		R		
E	N	E	E	T	H		A			A		
N	G	K				G	E	S	U	N	D	
		E						I			K	
							I					
						T						

⑪ a. Shut up! **b.** I'm fed up. **c.** He lives like a king. **d.** The truth will come out. **e.** Don't worry about it.

11. The genitive

① **a.** die Tasche des kleinen Mädchens **b.** das Auto eines reichen Mannes **c.** die Schulbücher der neuen Schüler **d.** der Stock einer alten Frau

② **a.** die Koffer von den deutschen Touristen **b.** das Fahrrad von dem kleinen Mädchen **c.** die Sporthalle von der neuen Schule **d.** der Plan von einem alten Flughafen

③ **a.** Peters Buch liegt auf dem Tisch. **b.** Kennst du Sabines neuen Freund? **c.** Der kleine Bruder von Paul ist in meiner Klasse. **d.** Ich habe der Frau von Richard eine Mail geschrieben.

④ **a.** Trotz **b.** Wegen **c.** Während **d.** Wegen

⑤ **Column 1:** der Student, den Studenten, dem Studenten, des Studenten **Column 2:** der Löwe, den Löwen, dem Löwen, des Löwen

⑥ **Column 1:** die Studenten, die Studenten, den Studenten, der Studenten **Column 2:** die Löwen, die Löwen, den Löwen, der Löwen

⑦ **a.** prince **b.** man (human being) **c.** bear **d.** policeman **e.** boy **f.** monkey **g.** composer **h.** raven **i.** hero

⑧ **a.** in die **b.** in c. nach **d.** in

⑨ **a.** der Engländer **b.** Afrika **c.** der Franzose **d.** Asien **e.** der Europäer **f.** Irland **g.** der Italiener **h.** Griechenland

⑩ **a.** Spanisch **b.** Chinesisch **c.** Englisch **d.** Japanisch **e.** Italienisch **f.** Russisch

12. Two-way prepositions

① **a.** in die **b.** in der **c.** am **d.** ans **e.** im **f.** auf der

② **a.** an **b.** auf **c.** in **d.** neben **e.** zwischen **f.** über

③ **a.** im Kino **b.** ins Bett **c.** ins Schwimmbad **d.** in der Zeitung **e.** in den falschen Bus **f.** im Internet **g.** in der Schule

④ **a.** gelegt **b.** setzen **c.** stehen **d.** hängt **e.** liegt

⑤ **a.** Häng **b.** gesessen **c.** stehe **d.** lag **e.** standen

⑥ **a.** du kämmst dich **b.** er/sie freut sich **c.** wir machen uns einen Tee **d.** ich setze mich

⑦ **a.** Ich habe keine Zeit, ich muss mich vorbereiten. **b.** Dreh dich nicht um! Er ist da. **c.** Sie hat sich sehr gut benommen. **d.** Wir haben uns im Urlaub (in den Ferien) gut erholt. **e.** Beeil(e) dich! Der Film beginnt in 5 Minuten / fängt in 5 Minuten an. **f.** Ich habe mich noch nicht angezogen.

⑧ 1g – 2b – 3f – 4e – 5c – 6a – 7h – 8d

⑨ **a.** oben **b.** Drinnen / nach draußen **c.** links / rechts **d.** von rechts **e.** nach hinten

⑩ **a.** komme **b.** geradeaus **c.** Biegen **d.** Nehmen **e.** verlaufen / verfahren **f.** Richtung

⑪

					K							
K	M	B	S	C	H	W	I	M	M	B	A	D
R	U	A			R			R		Ä		
A	S	C	H	U	L	E		C		C		
N	E	N			H			K		K		
K	U	H		T	H	E	A	T	E	R		
E	M	O						E				
N		F						E				
H					P			I		K		
A	P	O	T	H	E	K	E		O			I
U							S	T	A	D	I	O	N
S	U	P	E	R	M	A	R	K	T			O

13. Word order

① **a.** Mein Sohn zieht im Mai um. / Im Mai zieht mein Sohn um. **b.** Er ist heute losgefahren. / Heute ist er losgefahren. **c.** Du kannst nächste Woche bei mir wohnen. / Nächste Woche kannst du bei mir wohnen.

② **a.** (…), ob das Wetter am Wochenende schön wird. **b.** (…), ob ihr Bruder am Samstag mitkommen kann. **c.** (…), ob er deine Mutter angerufen hat.

③ **a.** Wenn es keinen Verkehr gibt, kommen wir pünktlich an. **b.** Ich möchte meine Mutter anrufen, bevor wir anfangen. **c.** Nachdem wir Sabine zum Bahnhof gebracht haben, können wir dich nach Hause fahren.

④ **a.** obwohl **b.** bevor **c.** dass **d.** damit **e.** bis **f.** wenn **g.** ob

⑤ **a.** weil **b.** Da **c.** denn **d.** weil

⑥ **a.** schneeweiß (snow white) **b.** hellgrün (light green) **c.** rabenschwarz (jet black) **d.** hausgemacht (homemade) **e.** lebensfroh (full of the joys of life) **f.** seekrank (seasick)

⑦ 1g Stroh / dumm 2d Kinder *(pl.)* / leicht 3b Riese / groß 4f pflegen (Pflege) / leicht 5c Farben *(pl.)* / blind 6a Bild / hübsch 7e Feder / leicht

⑧ **a.** am Apparat **b.** zurückrufen **c.** verwählt **d.** Telefonnummer / Vorwahl **e.** Nachricht **f.** Hallo **g.** Auf Wiederhören

⑨ **a.** Fernsehen **b.** Radio **c.** Buch **d.** Brief **e.** Zeitung **f.** Zeitschrift **g.** Nachrichten **h.** Tagesschau

⑩ **a.** das **b.** das **c.** der **d.** die / das **e.** die **f.** die / das **g.** der **h.** die **i.** die **j.** die **k.** der / das **l.** die **m.** das **n.** das

⑪ 1d – 2e – 3f – 4a – 5b – 6g – 7c

14. Modal verbs

① **a.** soll **b.** musste **c.** Darf **d.** dürfen **e.** kann **f.** Möchten **g.** kann **h.** Weißt

② **a.** darf **b.** kann **c.** will **d.** möchte **e.** muss **f.** soll

③ **a.** wiederholen **b.** rufen **c.** ausfüllen **d.** buchstabieren **e.** warten **f.** halten

④ 1c – 2e – 3b – 4a – 5f – 6d

⑤ **a.** Sie darf weder ausgehen noch Freunde einladen. **b.** Du musst ihn entweder heute Abend oder morgen Mittag anrufen. **c.** Sie kann sowohl Italienisch als auch/wie auch Englisch. **d.** Ich möchte entweder ein Schokoladeneis oder einen Schokoladenkuchen.

⑥ **a.** der Zug **b.** das Flugzeug **c.** der Wagen **d.** das Schiff

⑦ **a.** crossroad/intersection **b.** accident **c.** traffic **d.** traffic jam **e.** traffic light **f.** petrol/gas station

8 **a.** Haltestelle **b.** Autobus **c.** U-Bahn **d.** Station **e.** Motorrad **f.** Straßenbahn **g.** Autobahn **h.** Straße

9

```
F
L A U F E N
I
E   R
G E H E N
E   N  S
N   N  E
    E  G
  L A N D E N
    L
F A H R E N
```

15. Verbs with prefixes

1 **a.** verstanden **b.** gewonnen **c.** verboten **d.** empfehlen **e.** erzählt **f.** bekommst **g.** entdeckt **h.** benommen

2 **a.** einladen **b.** aufgeräumt **c.** Bringen (…) mit **d.** angerufen **e.** steigen (…) aus **f.** vorbeigegangen **g.** zurückgekommen

3 **a.** l **b.** S **c.** S **d.** l **e.** l **f.** S **g.** l **h.** l **i.** l **j.** S **k.** S **l.** l

4 **a.** aufmachen **b.** angefangen **c.** vergeht **d.** hören **e.** besuchen **f.** durchgefallen

5 **Verb:** abfahren, ankommen, bestellen, unterschreiben **Noun:** die Erklärung, die Erzählung, der Anfang, die Wiederholung

6 **a.** an **b.** um **c.** aus **d.** zugenommen **e.** abnehmen

7 **a.** her **b.** hin **c.** hin **d.** her **e.** her **f.** hin

8 **a.** aber **b.** aber **c.** sondern **d.** sondern **e.** aber **f.** sondern

9 1d – 2e – 3a – 4f – 5g – 6c – 7b

10 1e – 2g – 3f – 4b – 5d – 6c – 7a

11 1d – 2e – 3c – 4g – 5a – 6b – 7f

12 1a ausgegeben 2d – 3e bezahlt 4b überwiesen 5c verdient

13

```
R   G E L D
E E
B I L L I G
C D     B
H B     A
R E C H N U N G
U       K
T   A
T E U E R
L   M
```

14 **a.** Time is money. **b.** The best things in life are free. / Money isn't everything. ('Better a man without money than money without man'). **c.** Money can't buy happiness. **d.** He's rolling ('swimming') in money.

16. Prepositional verbs

1 **a.** für **b.** nach **c.** um **d.** von **e.** zu **f.** über **g.** über **h.** für

2 **a.** dich **b.** dich **c.** den **d.** meine **e.** dich **f.** eine **g.** dich **h.** der

3 **a.** danach **b.** daran **c.** an ihn **d.** An sie **e.** daran

4 **a.** Woran **b.** An wen **c.** Wofür **d.** In wen **e.** Womit

5 **a.** stolz **b.** einverstanden **c.** zufrieden **d.** fertig **e.** weit **f.** freundlich

6 1g – 2e – 3b – 4a – 5f – 6d – 7h – 8c

7 **a.** Ich habe gehört/erfahren, dass Sabine geheiratet hat. **b.** Ich möchte Deutsch lernen. **c.** Sie lehrt ihn Tennis spielen. / Sie bringt ihm Tennnis spielen bei. **d.** Ich lerne besser am Morgen als am Nachmittag. **e.** Sie lehrt die Ausländer Deutsch. / Sie bringt den Ausländern Deutsch bei.

8 1f – 2e – 3b – 4c – 5d – 6a

9 **a.** Flughafen **b.** Gepäck **c.** Fenster / Gang **d.** Flug **e.** Bahnhof / Gleis **f.** Ermäßigung **g.** Fahrkarte

10

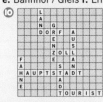

```
      L
    A N G
  D O R F  A
        E  U
        N  S
        Z O L L
        E  A
F       S  N
H A U P T S T A D T
N       A  D
E       T O U R I S T
```

11 **a.** the Black Forest **b.** Lake Constance **c.** Cologne Cathedral **d.** the Bavarian Forest **e.** the Brandenburg Gate **f.** the Berlin Wall **g.** the Baltic Sea **h.** the North Sea

12 **a.** Reise **b.** Ferien **c.** Urlaub **d.** Ausweis **e.** Reisepass **f.** Zuschlag **g.** Flugticket **h.** Aufenthalt

17. Infinitives

1 **a.** – **b.** – **c.** zu **d.** – **e.** zu **f.** zu **g.** –

2 **a.** anstatt (…) zu **b.** um zu / um zu **c.** Ohne (…) zu **d.** ohne (…) zu **e.** Um (…) zu **f.** ohne zu

3 1f – 2d – 3g – 4h – 5b – 6e – 7a – 8c

4 **a.** Stundenlanges Warten … **b.** Wundermedikament zum Abnehmen **c.** Wenig Essen … **d.** Das Einkaufen ist … **e.** Beim Fahren eingeschlafen

5 **a.** Ich brauche ein Glas zum Trinken. **b.** Das ist eine schöne Wiese zum Spielen. **c.** Vor dem Laufen mache ich ein paar Sportübungen. **d.** Ich komme nach dem Trainieren. **e.** Er braucht einen Stock zum Gehen.

6 1h – 2e – 3f – 4c – 5a – 6g – 7d – 8b

7 **a.** fallen **b.** schlagen **c.** brechen **d.** heben **e.** springen **f.** verlieren **g.** ziehen **h.** schneiden **i.** steigen

8 **a.** Wir sind nach Berlin gefahren, um meine Tante zu besuchen. **b.** Wir planen, nach Indien zu reisen. **c.** Ich werde früher aus dem Büro gehen, um ihn abzuholen. **d.** Ich freue mich, mit der ganzen Familie eine Woche in Wien zu verbringen. **e.** Er betrat den Raum, ohne mich zu grüßen. **f.** Anstatt ein Geschenk zu kaufen, werde ich ihm Geld geben. **g.** (no comma)

9 **a.** Hör auf **b.** anhalten **c.** hielt (…) an **d.** blieb (…) stehen **e.** hört (…) auf

10 **a.** Ich höre auf zu spielen. **b.** Bleib stehen! Ich kann nicht so schnell gehen. **c.** Halt an! Es ist rot. **d.** Hör auf, Schokolade zu essen. **e.** Der Schiedsrichter stoppte das Spiel / hat das Spiel gestoppt.

11 1e – 2b – 3a – 4f – 5d – 6c

18. Showing possession

1 **a.** mein **b.** eure **c.** ihr **d.** deine **e.** seine **f.** unser

2 **a.** seinen **b.** meine **c.** ihre **d.** deine **e.** euren **f.** unsere

3 **a.** Sabine ist bei ihrem Freund. **b.** Paul ist auch bei ihrem Freund. **c.** Paul ruft seinen Freund an. **d.** Paul ruft seine Freundin an. **e.** Sabine ruft ihre Freundin an. **f.** Sabine ruft seinen Freund an. **g.** Sabine ruft seine Freundin an. **h.** Paul ist auch bei ihrer Freundin.

4 **a.** seine **b.** uns(e)rer **c.** eu(e)re **d.** dein(e)s **e.** meine **f.** eu(e)re

5 **a.** ihrem **b.** deinen **c.** eu(e)re **d.** Ihrer **e.** seinem

6 **a.** erst **b.** nur **c.** erst **d.** nur **e.** erst **f.** nur

7 **a.** (There is still a long way to go.) / (We only had to drive for 100 km.) **b.** (He's going to write a lot more.) / (He only wrote one page.) **c.** (He won't arrive before tomorrow.) / (He'll be here only one day, tomorrow.)

8 **a.** Ich habe sie (am) Anfang der Woche getroffen. **b.** Sie ist dreißig. **c.** Am Ende war es besser. **d.** Er arbeitet seit Mitte Dezember. **e.** Sie haben Ende Juni geheiratet. **f.** Es steht am Anfang des Buches.

9 **a.** It's over. **b.** I was there from start to finish. **c.** I'm completely exhausted. **d.** Every beginning is hard. **e.** I could eat forever. **f.** There's no end to it.

10 **a.** Nichte / Neffe / Neffe **b.** Schwiegermutter / Schwiegervater / Schwiegereltern **c.** Schwägerin / Schwager **d.** Onkel / Tante **e.** Cousine / Cousin **f.** Großeltern **g.** Urgroßvater **h.** Enkelin / Enkel **i.** Enkelkinder

Panel **a.** die Braut (the bride) **b.** der Bräutigam (the groom) **c.** der Ehering (the wedding ring) **d.** das Brautkleid (the wedding dress) **e.** das Brautpaar (the bride and groom)

11 **a.** heiraten **b.** Heiratsantrag **c.** die Scheidungsrate / Hochzeiten / Ehe **d.** bekommen ihr erstes Kind **e.** die Liebe auf den ersten Blick

19. Relative pronouns

1 **a.** den **b.** wo **c.** den **d.** denen **e.** das

2 **a.** Das Bett, wo ich schlafe, ist nicht breit. **b.** Die Stadt, woher ich komme, liegt im Norden. **c.** Das Restaurant, wohin ich gehen wollte, hat zu. **d.** Das ist ein kleines Kino, wo gute Filme laufen.

3 **a.** deren **b.** dessen **c.** deren **d.** dessen

4 **a.** Peter ist ein Schüler, mit dem ich sehr zufrieden bin. **b.** Kennst du einen Schauspieler, dessen Name mit D anfängt/beginnt? **c.** Das ist der Film, der einen Oscar gewonnen hat. **d.** Er wohnt in Heidelberg, wo ich 5 Jahre lang gearbeitet habe.

5 **a.** Was **b.** Wer **c.** was **d.** was **e.** das **f.** Wer **g.** was

6 **a.** Die **b.** denen **c.** Den **d.** den **e.** Der

7 **a.** kommt vor **b.** geschehen/passiert **c.** passiert **d.** schaffen **e.** kommt vor

8 **a.** Es kommt vor, dass es im Mai schneit. **b.** Was ist dir passiert? **c.** Wann ist das passiert/geschehen? **d.** Super (Toll), du hast es geschafft! **e.** Er lässt das nie geschehen/passieren.

9 **a.** 1, 10 **b.** 2, 4, 5, 9, 13 **c.** 7, 8, 11, 12, 13 **d.** 3, 6, 8, 13

10 **a.** die → heat **b.** das → climate **c.** der → rain **d.** die → temperature **e.** der → snow **f.** das → black ice **g.** dor → hail **h.** der → wind **i.** der → lightning **j.** das → weather **k.** der → rainbow **l.** der → thunder

11

							P	
							L	
							A	
		S	T	E	R	N		
				R		E		
		S		D		T		
	W	O	L	K	E			
		N		N				
		N						
H	I	M	M	E	L			
	O			U				
	N			F				
	D			T				

12 **a.** Januar **b.** Februar **c.** März **d.** April **e.** Mai **f.** Juni **g.** Juli **h.** August **i.** September **j.** Oktober **k.** November **l.** Dezember **m.** Frühling **n.** Sommer **o.** Herbst **p.** Winter

20. Making comparisons

1 **Line 1:** Paul ist so dick wie ich. Paul ist dicker als ich. Paul ist der dickste/am dicksten von allen. **Line 2:** Sabine ist so schlank wie ich. Sabine ist schlanker als ich. Sabine ist die schlankste/am schlanksten von allen. **Line 3:** Ana ist so schnell wie ich. Ana ist schneller als ich. Ana ist die schnellste/am schnellsten von allen.

2 **a.** kleinste **b.** billiger **c.** längste **d.** höchste **e.** früheren **f.** am meisten

3 **a.** teurer **b.** hübscheste **c.** am weitesten **d.** dunkleren **e.** ältesten **f.** süßesten

4 **a.** Ich gehe gern zu Fuß. **b.** Fährst du lieber mit dem Zug oder mit dem Auto? **c.** Ich habe Ana lieber als Susi. **d.** Am liebsten bleibe ich zu Hause. **e.** Ich hätte gern Herrn Müller.

5 **a.** lieber / am liebsten **b.** gern **c.** am liebsten **d.** lieber

6

			S	C	H	A	T	Z
						A		
		M				S		
B	Ö					S		
E	G					E		
L	I	E	B	L	I	N	G	
I		N		I				
E				E				
B				B				
T		L	I	E	B	E	N	

7 **a.** weniger **b.** mehr **c.** mehr **d.** weniger

8 **a.** Was für ein Auto hast du? **b.** Was für Bücher liest du gern? **c.** Mit was für einer Maschine bist du geflogen? **d.** In was für ein Restaurant gehst du lieber?

9 **a.** Welche (Linie) nimmst du (meistens)? **b.** Auf welcher (Schule) warst du? **c.** Welche (Zeitung) liest du? **d.** Zu welchem (Bäcker) gehst du (oft)?

10 **a.** Für welche Zeitung arbeitest du? **b.** Mit welchem Lehrer lernst du Deutsch? **c.** In welcher Firma arbeitet er? **d.** Ich weiß nicht, welchen Zug er genommen hat. **e.** Welche Bücher sind für mich?

11 **a.** böse **b.** schnell **c.** dick **d.** trocken **e.** leise **f.** sauer **g.** glücklich **h.** leicht

12 **a.** gesund / krank **b.** stark / schwach **c.** fleißig / faul **d.** intelligent / dumm

21. Numbers

1 **a.** siebzehn Komma fünfundzwanzig **b.** achthundertsechzig **c.** eine Million vierhunderttausend

2 **a.** zum zehnten Mal **b.** im einundzwanzigsten Jahrhundert **c.** Papst Paul der Sechste

3 **a.** Montag **b.** Dienstag **c.** Mittwoch **d.** Donnerstag **e.** Freitag **f.** Samstag **g.** Sonntag

4 **a.** Ich bin am sechzehnten Juli angekommen. **b.** Heute ist der neunundzwanzigste Februar. **c.** Ich war im Mai 2012 in Berlin. **d.** Sie haben am Samstag, den/dem fünfzehnten Mai geheiratet. **e.** Wir fahren an/zu Weihnachten weg.

Fantastisch! You've reached the end of this workbook. Now it's time to assess how you did by counting up the icons of each type for all the lessons. Make sure that you've put the sub-totals from each lesson in the boxes below, and then add them up to find the total number for each of the three icons.

	☺	☻	☹		☺	☻	☹
1. The present tense				12. Two-way prepositions			
2. The imperative				13. Word order			
3. The present perfect				14. Modal verbs			
4. The simple past				15. Verbs with prefixes			
5. The future				16. Prepositional verbs			
6. The subjunctive II				17. Infinitives			
7. The passive voice				18. Showing possession			
8. Nouns & the nominative				19. Relative pronouns			
9. The accusative				20. Making comparisons			
10. The dative				21. Numbers			
11. The genitive							

☺ ☻ ☹

Total (all lessons) ....

Which icon has the highest total?

☺   ☻   ☹

Gratuliere! You have mastered the basics of German and are ready to move on to the next level!

Nicht schlecht... but there's room for improvement. Go back and redo the exercises that gave you trouble, reviewing the information if necessary.

Noch einmal! You're a bit rusty ... Go through the workbook again and redo the exercises, reviewing the information first.

Credits: Illustrations / © MS

Designed by: MediaSarbacane
Layout: Violeta Cabal

© 2016 Assimil
Legal deposit: February 2016
Publication no.: 3514
ISBN: 978-2-7005-0713-3
www.assimil.com
Printed in Slovenia by DZS Grafik